Turning Trauma into Triumph

Jennifer Gilmour

Steph,

Thank you for your support with the kickstarter campaign and for helping bring this book to life. Also, thank you for your ongoing support and friendship. I love you! We've got this next chapter!

Together we are louder!

Jennifer G vvv
Nov 2024

Copyright

First published in 2024 Jennifer Gilmour

Copyright © Jennifer Gilmour 2024

The rights of the author have been asserted in accordance with Sections 77 of the Copyright, Designs, and Patents Act, 1988.

All rights reserved.

No part of this book may be reproduced (including photocopying or storing in any medium by electronic means and whether or not transiently or incidentally to some other use of this publication) without the written permission of the copyright holder except in accordance with the provisions of the Copyright, Designs, and Patents Act 1988. Applications for the Copyright holder's written permission to reproduce any part of this publication should be addressed to the publishers.

This is work of non-fiction however some names have been changed to protect the identities of those mentioned.

A CIP catalogue record for this book is available from the British Library ISBN 978-1-9999647-4-0 (Neilsen UK).

Published by Pict Publishing

Dedication

This book is dedicated to my very best friend Bianca Levesley.

You have shown me what true friendship is (judgement free and consistent), you've taught me that inner happiness is the most important kind (I don't need to find this in someone else) and that I can build my own support circle with the right people (they are my true family).

I can't imagine doing life without you.

Contents

Introduction	VI
1. Insight Into My Lived Experiences	1
2. Reflecting	24
3. Recovery And Healing	40
4. Learning Through Self-Education And Courses	63
5. Mental Health	84
6. Life After Domestic Abuse And Healthy Relationships	97
7. Support	124
8. Important Phone Numbers And Supportive Websites	141
9. Where to next?	143
10. Acknowledgements	148
11. In memory of Paul	150
12. Supporters, Backers And Pledgers	152
13. About The Author	155
14. References	157
15. Also By Jennifer Gilmour	159

Introduction

It has been eleven years since I fled the abusive relationship I was trapped in for several years. Over those years I have educated myself on domestic abuse and how it has had a long lasting impact on me. I have shared blog posts about my journey, I have had to live with post separation abuse, I have gone on recovery programmes, assisted a recovery programme with anecdotes, written best selling books, created a community of survivors and I have made it through each day. I initially wanted to mark the decade that I had struggled through but I'm here a year on from that anniversary with an adapted collection of blog posts and articles that I have produced over the last five years.

I was proud to receive an award for my blog - Most Informative Blogger (Blogger Bash Awards 2018). It was one of my most encouraging moments in the early stages of my writing journey and it instilled some confidence in me to continue my path to raise awareness through my lived experiences. On a personal note, my blog certainly gave me that nostalgic feeling of journalling which I did for many years in my teens and young adulthood.

My blog has been recommended to read at events, I have received lots of positive feedback from readers from different backgrounds and professions. I finally made the step in bringing it to life so I hope you find it both insightful and educational as you read through my therapeutic writing journey.

The perfectionist within me wants to let you know that it was difficult to create structure for this book, I originally started with oldest to newest because this would have shown the progression of my mindset. I have created various categories that you can head straight to if you wish and within the category the entries are placed in publication order. To help, I have added the date each piece was written so you can follow along with ease. The entries have been kept as close to the original piece as possible with minor edits for typos and that's why each chapter closes with a reflection piece written especially for this book.

You can read this book in any way you wish because each entry can be read in isolation to each other, check out the contents and flick to a category you are drawn to, read from start to finish or back to front.

Readers, please keep yourself safe whilst you're reading this book. There is a section toward the back of this book with support numbers and websites should you need to speak with anyone regarding any challenges that come to the surface.

Content warning: Controlling behaviour, sexual violence, physical abuse, emotional abuse, child abuse, mental health struggles, attempted suicide, medical conditions and sexuality.

Insight Into My Lived Experiences

Scars will fade [March 2016]

I was particularly excited when I became a blogger for the Huffington Post and it filled me with confidence to think about how to articulate sharing my story in short snippets and not as a whole.

My first post was about how there can be a good life waiting for you once you admit to and address being in an abusive relationship. I thought it was important for readers to know that even after the passage of days, months and years that there are still moments I relive my time in such a relationship and that there are still times when I find the every day life hard. There are every day challenges that take time to heal and some, I am sad to say, will never fully repair. It is like a wound – your blood clots and your skin knits together, it then becomes a scab which could be there a few weeks and then there's a scar left – that scar will fade but there will always be a mark. You know the story behind that scar and you carry it around everywhere you go and when someone asks, you choose whether or not to tell the story behind it or whether it's too painful to think back and so leave it untouched. The memory is always there and time does help but you are reminded of it every time you notice that particular scar.

Life after domestic abuse

I used to wonder if I would ever have a life. In fact I wondered this every day for the five long, lonely years that I lived in a domestic abusive relationship. In the end I didn't care because I was so numb, but here I am now and I want to share with you a snippet of my story.

If you are wondering why someone didn't intervene, let me tell you that there are were no scars; there were no bruises, in fact there was no obvious physical evidence that anything was wrong. The scars and bruising were real though... in my mind. I wasn't hit or kicked, in fact sometimes I wish I had been as that would have brought some sort of end to the crazy mindset the man I thought loved me persuaded me to believe about myself.

When we first got together things were normal. Well, I think they were but as I look back I am no longer sure what normal was in that relationship. To excuse his behaviour, I convinced myself that he was just showing an over-protective love as opposed to obsession and control.

I fell for his easy charm and within a few months became pregnant with my first child, and things changed a lot from there. The episodes of abuse, which had been infrequent at first, became monthly events. To begin with they would consist of interrogating me in the middle of the night, not letting me sleep and making me sleep on the floor despite being pregnant. Other behaviours involved locking me in the house and throwing things at me. I had no control over any money and as a consequence the debts mounted. I didn't have my family close by as they live on the other side of the country- I felt alone and trapped. Life progressed in this way until eventually I wasn't allowed to go out to work. By this time I had two children and felt isolated and unsure. What could I do? I had no money, few friends, no independence and low self-esteem despite having a university diploma.

I felt I had to do something so I created a business working from home because surely he couldn't argue with that? Or could he?

As I look back, I realise that if it wasn't for some business friends I made at that time I wouldn't have found the confidence to change this downward cycle which imprisoned me. As the debts mounted he agreed that I could get a part time, temporary job for the Christmas season. I became friends with the Manager at my new place of employment. There was something about this man which made me feel able to trust him with what was happening in my life. As I opened up to him, he was concerned to hear of events that were happening in my life and tried to convince me that these were not normal in a relationship.

Thankfully my new friend decided to help me and he became my hero who I could talk to before going back home where I had to act like nothing was wrong. I decided that, with my two children, I was going to leave the husband who was abusing me and move back to my family on the other side of the country. My friend decided he was going to give up his job and move with me and the children. I may have made this sound easy but I can assure you this was very challenging both emotionally and practically. We did it though, and that friend is now my husband and we have both my children and a baby of our own living all under one roof. I couldn't be happier.

The scars of domestic abuse are often hidden from view but as my confidence and happiness have soared, I have realised that there is help out there and there is a way back to freedom.

released a novel based on the less well-known aspects of domestic abuse. I want to help other women to believe in themselves and find a way out if they feel trapped as I did. I want to help them to take that first step to freedom. I have learnt that the hardest part is not with the breaking up, it's the life after - the weeks, the months, the years of healing from the hurt and emotional trauma from the abuse.

I know that many have and continue to relate with the story I tell through my book, "Isolation Junction" and I hope in this way to raise awareness of this silent but deadly and insidious behaviour which ruins the lives of so many.

Fight Against Domestic Violence [June 2017]

I first met my abuser at work. He was quite flirty with me and would pay me compliments. I was flattered. Over the weeks we became good friends and would often laugh and joke together. One evening we went out with friends and I realised he was interested in me as more than a friend. I was a young student living far from home and his attention felt good. Our relationship moved on quickly but after a relatively short time, looking back, the signs were there. He began to get jealous of any men who smiled at me, talked to me or even looked at me. Looking back I should have ended things because he would accuse me of not taking the relationship seriously. I I felt I couldn't break things off because I didn't want my family to think that I had ended a previous long term relationship for a mere fling Besides, I wanted to show that I had a good moral compass. I stuck with the relationship but things got worse and then I fell pregnant. I believed I should stay with the baby's father and I didn't want my child to be the victim of a broken home and I certainly didn't want to look a failure. I became convinced that I could fix any problems that we had and convinced myself that his controlling behaviour wasn't his fault but was as a result the way he was brought up. However, as I learnt to my cost, I couldn't fix things. There was no excuse for his controlling behaviour and things continued to get worse until he decided that I should leave our marital home. By now I had two children and he and his family spat at me as I left (minus my children). I was distraught but thankfully help came from an unexpected quarter. A new friend, told me quite clearly that the kind of behaviour I was being subjected to was simply unacceptable and was extremely unhealthy. He was the person who helped to lift the scales from my eyes regarding what was happening in my relationship and was the catalyst who helped me to move on both mentally and physically and to seek professional help and support. Since that time I have worked hard to be an advocate for women in coercive and controlling relationships and last year published my novel 'Isolation Junction'- a fictional story based on the real life facts surrounding coercive control. I am now happily married with three children and live in the U.K. and I am a Jamberry consultant.

My reality as a woman... IWD...[March 2018]

How do I feel as a woman?

I love and I hate it.

I hate it because being a woman isn't always easy in fact it can be completely unbearable at times. Most of my own issues were when I was growing up, I was either wolf whistled at for wearing a skirt or I was picked on for having no breasts. I actually decided to go tomboy for a while and in fact I wished I was a boy back then, at the time I didn't know why but looking back I remember it was for the lifestyle they have (or what I perceived it was).

Of course when I entered the relationship that was abusive I was treated like a 1950's house wife. I was stripped of being able to feel feminine or the woman I wanted to be. Towards the end I was a robot living by the many standards and rules he had coded me to obey, a sad life to live with no voice.

So whilst we have been celebrating International Women's Day we also need to be thinking about all those women in a refuge, all those women in abusive relationships, all the women who are survivors and all those women who speak out against domestic abuse.

I love being a woman in 2018 because I am able to speak out and voice what needs to be heard. I love that I can dress how I would like, be my own character, have a different sense of freedom, let's face it I can be who I want to be.

This evening I am asking you not only to think but also to stand with me, stand with me to help block the road to Isolation Junction. Isolation Junction is a place no one should visit, no one should be made to feel like they have no one and no where to turn.

How many will have been in an abusive relationship? How many people are in an abusive relationship?

1 in 4 women and 1 in 6 men

What he used to call me [July 2018]

A post popped up in my street team just the other day and boy was it a trigger! Every time I see anything to do with Batman's the Joker I can remember the humiliation and the cruel things he used to say to me.

Wonder why I always hide my mouth when I smile? Why I try not to show my teeth? I wonder if those around me had ever noticed before?

I don't even really want to write it here because of fear of others using it and seeing it as a weakness, the truth is it doesn't hurt me it just causes me to remember what my ex-abuser used to do with cruel laughing and pointing at me.

I bet your thinking - cut to the chase! Say it! Tell us what he said! But I'm sure your reaction will be, what! Why do you think on it anymore? You know it's not true! You are beautiful! Or perhaps you're thinking he's right, that's my true fear and drawing attention to it here could only make it worse.

BUT I'm going to tell you because I know that someone out there will relate to this. The comment he used was something I shake my head at now, I don't know why he fixated on it. Perhaps he destined for me never to smile again.

Ok... here goes! Every time I smile I have this BEAMING smile. It takes over my mouth and in my head it makes others smile. To him he used to laugh, point and almost used to wee himself because I smiled. He even asked me to stop smiling. He said at each edge of my mouth it was like I was cut to make my smile wider like the Joker. For years it was something he would come back to over and over again, he laughed so much his eyes would water. Can you imagine how I felt?

My husband tells me I am truly beautiful and to smile more. He's stuck the plasters on my emotional wounds, helped me to regain my confidence. It's in confidence I post this. Because if you are being humiliated like this, it isn't normal, if you tell someone it's hurtful and it makes you not want to smile (or refrain from whatever it is) then it is cruel and its a sign of an unhealthy relationship. Why would the person who says they love you want to upset you like this?

It haunts me now and I'm sure if he read this he would be happy with himself. BUT I feel I have my smile back, I'm happy and I will show my pearly white teeth so that others can smile with me. It's a smile I'm not going to hide. So if you see me tell me to smile, I'll smile with you! You can't hide happiness or recovery.

I feel like my smile says many things but most of all it reveals how far I have come and that I allow myself to be happy again.

My Experiences of Sleep Deprivation [December 2019]

One night I was falling to sleep when I suddenly saw a dark figure standing over me. I blinked and realised my mind was playing tricks on me and it was just the way the light was shining through the curtains. It shook me up because I remembered how fearful going to sleep could be.

I haven't spoken much about the sleep deprivation I experienced throughout my abusive relationship and so I thought I would share some of what I went through. It was progressive throughout the years I was with him.

It started with arguments that he chose to have with me in the middle of the night. I'm not just talking about before bed but being woken up in the middle of the night by him shaking me to initiate an argument. Usually because of his paranoid and over jealous state that he had worked himself up into.

There were subtle things like me wanting to go to bed as it was late but he didn't want to be left awake and I was called boring, not interesting and old for doing so. I knew that him calling me boring would lead to him looking elsewhere for attention, I felt pressured to stay up and I forced myself to be able to. I stayed up until midnight at the earliest, it became a struggle for me when I became a new mum.

Sleep became a luxury toward the end of that relationship and I was lucky to get a solid block in a night. I did have two children in the mix and obviously the duties I had as a mum took place. A lot of the time I felt like a single mum because it was an old fashioned relationship of me tending to the children. Incidents occurred to which I felt I had to get up so that they weren't put through any of his shouting, it wasn't their fault that they had usual child needs.

The problem with this was that I'd kick myself if I didn't wake up before him and that was usually through exhaustion. I became ultra-sensitive to hearing them and found I was waking multiple times a night when I wasn't needed.

There were times I woke up and he was standing over me, he claimed to be watching me whilst I slept. I found it disturbing and I was always concerned when this happened. I can only remember a handful of occasions but there were other times I could hear him pacing around the bed.

I remember some occasions I was made to sleep on the floor when I was pregnant and other times I had water thrown on my face.

A lot of this led to me experiencing nightmares, some of them were extreme about been taken away by aliens. I had always experienced vivid dreams and I can wake up and remember the senses and detail to them. When I confided in my partner at the time he went along with it and told me it could have happened. It became a game to him that he could use about the dark figure next to the bed as the alien that came. I have to be honest and say there was a time I considered this could be real, his involvement made me think I was experiencing something. Looking back I think how silly I was but I can also understand just what situation I was in the depth of and that his manipulation was at full effect. He was the dark figure next to the bed and this was something he could use as an illusion.

I remember being so tired that as soon as I would hit the pillow I would be fast asleep. But that wasn't safe either.

After the relationship had ended I suffered from nightmares and my new partner could recall when I wasn't in a good place in my mindset because I would talk or scream out in my sleep. Usually, it was linked to further abuse or incidents with my ex.

Sleep can still be a tricky one for me depending on what projects I am working on and what I remember from my experiences. I try and work it through and leave the day on a positive note to try and override it all.

Controlling someone's sleep is a form of abuse, one which is cruel and can have an impact on your health.

The unsettling familiarity of social distancing [April 2020]

We are now into the third week of social distancing in the UK, I haven't stopped with the amount I do online or the direction I am going in. I have had to wait on a lot of calls to try and get refunds for train tickets and hotel bookings though. I have done a few interviews in regards to the work I do and what lockdown means for those in abusive relationships, you can imagine the pressure cooker of a situation for those couples and families.

This whole experience has given me a lot to think about but there's something I do want to shed light on. I have been several years out of the relationship with my ex-abuser and I still find myself working on sections of my life, one by one. There were certain things he embedded in me to be sensitive too and they are difficult to unpick due to the natural way in which my brain works, Rock Pool's recovery toolkit course taught me that some of these are NAT's (Negative Automatic Thinking).

I felt that over the last year I had started to understand my freedom with life in the sense of traveling and going to different events. It may seem like such a simple to task but I assure you that every time I would leave home and be away from my children, a wave of guilt and a rush to get everything done as fast as I could to get home would come over me. It stems from when I was with my ex abuser, he would lock me away from the world (emotionally and physically).

By the end of that relationship:

I got used to staying in my home

I hadn't visited my home city of Hull for two years

I couldn't see friends

I only went out when I was allowed

I abided by the rules I was set

I was isolated, social distancing for me is an unsettling familiarity and I am sure I am not the only person with lived experiences feeling like this right now. There's a lot more depth than the small list I have created above but it gives you an idea.

If you haven't been in an abusive relationship but are feeling the frustration of lockdown, perhaps now you can start to think about how it must be to live a life of restrictions. Its nowhere near close to the reality of an abusive relationship but I have seen plenty of posts about how its driving people 'crazy', people are drinking or eating more. Ultimately they are finding a way to cope like most of the world at the moment. Back then, I coped by accepting the situation I was in despite the feeling of it been an invisible prison and without an obvious or easy escape.

Right now I am working hard on looking after myself and hoping to come up with something to help others online. It's important that I do this because I really value the freedom in meeting with others, social distancing is not natural or easy. Let me know if there's something I can help you with.

For now, you can check out my 'life after abuse' mini-series of videos that are around 10 minutes each and look at isolation, support, recovery and healthy relationships. Available on my YouTube channel or on Instagram on IGTV.

I want to also mention my debut novel Isolation Junction, it's called that because I was isolated from the world. It is free to read on Kindle Unlimited, as well as my second publication Clipped Wings. Both equally important books that have helped others understand what it might be like to be in an abusive relationship, some have fled relationships and others have passed the book to someone it may help.

Stay safe and if you need some help or support please don't hesitate to get in touch.

The truth about my weight [August 2020]

For years I have struggled with a balance with my weight and for years I have Yo Yo dieted, I am sure like many others out there. I wanted to share why this happens with me and the deeper rooted trauma I have to overcome.

Whilst I was in my abusive relationship, my weight was an issue, it wasn't a problem for me but it was for him. Before meeting him I was fairly happy with my weight and my body image in general but all that was going to change. The harsh part for me is that I was actually a lot slimmer back then compared to me now.

At first, it was subtle hints;

Are you sure you want that chocolate?

Aren't you full?

You are going to need to work that off

But it changed to be more obvious and I started to cover myself up. I would wear clothes that were too big for me, I wouldn't let him see me naked and would always wear an oversized shirt when having sex. The subtle remarks had clearly started to tackle my subconscious and that's just how he worked me over the years, it didn't appear obvious and it made it look like it was my choice.

As time went on it became more obvious and I got more and more stressed until one day he said whilst laughing; "You've got more rollbacks then Asda".

It was already coming to the end of the relationship by the time the obvious comments and statements were coming in. One day he had gone shopping and said to me when he came back with a bag of clothes; "I asked the lady in the shop which tops would cover up your tummy the most because I know you're self conscious about it".

I was shocked about this in particular and remember feeling ashamed of myself. I had two young children and had been diagnosed with a brain adenoma in my pituitary gland, the last thing I was thinking was looking after my weight, I just wanted to feel better as I had intense migraines and would vomit in the mornings. But I couldn't let it shift my mind and the more the comments came in the more I didn't like the way I looked.

I bought myself an exercise bike and I would be on there for a minimum of an hour, I remember some times being on there for three hours in front of the TV. I felt I had something to prove and had a strange determination. Over the last weeks of the relationship and coming out, I lost 3 stone in 2 months. Looking back I do look good but I know why I was there and it wasn't for healthy reasons.

So, lets fast forward to the year 2020.

My goal for this year is to overcome my abuser's voice every time I walk into Asda. All I think about is that statement which is humorous in some ways and emotionally straining for me in other ways, I try and laugh it off but the reality is that it has had a long term effect on me. It is a part of the trauma of that relationship, I could avoid it and go to another supermarket chain but Asda happens to be on my doorstep. Avoiding it will only make it worse and so I overcome it each time I walk through the doors. But to truly overcome it, I need to do something about it.

The Recovery Toolkit has given me the tools to be able to overcome the trauma of that relationship and I have spent 6 years working through different triggers and silencing the abusers voice. I believe it would have been too much to do everything in one go.

To be able to overcome this, I need to be happy in myself and a weight I am confident with. I am four stones away from the photo taken in December 2013, but this isn't my goal. Lockdown hasn't made it easier as I put on a whole stone and a half, ouch. Lockdown wasn't easy for me and you can read some of my thoughts on this on my blog 'The unsettling familiarity of social distancing'. That doesn't mean I can't reach the goal or get a good start to it now, I haven't failed.

Start Goal: Lose 3 stone 7 lbs.

Change is happening, is it? [November 2020]

A few months have passed since I wrote "The Truth about my Weight" and I posted it because I thought sharing my personal challenge would help keep me motivated and accountable.

I have to admit, in the beginning, I was doing so well. In fact, I have lost over a stone in weight since I started the journey.

It all went wrong and I have felt like I have been in a fight in my brain ever since, fighting the urge for chocolate and bad food from the very beginning of the day. The next I am fighting putting anything in my mouth and am living on barely anything.

I have plateaued and haven't budged forward, I guess it was a stupid time to take on this challenge but I really felt ready for it. It happened before the news of the second lockdown but I fear going into it today and not having the gym available is like a final nail in the coffin.

I used to be able to have this control over myself and either stick to a diet or enjoy the time I was not on a diet. Maybe I am not ready for this kind of pressure considering the circumstances in my life? Maybe I need to push through and take this opportunity?

I do know one thing, I want to get this sorted and feel good about myself. I have seen the difference the first stone has made. But, the other side is that this was always going to be a fight because I am taking on all that past trauma. It can feel like he is with me all the time, every time I put something in my mouth, every time I exercise, every time I step on the scales. It's like a haunting.

Change is happening, is it? or perhaps not? I know that I have some medical challenges at the same time but this isn't an excuse. Perhaps I am not giving myself time to celebrate the first milestone of losing that stone.

I know that it has been on my mind because I have avoided it here and on my social media. So I am here to let you know I am normal and face challenges. I am truly a work in progress but I will be working hard to get to where I want to be, I am sure I will look back on this and be even prouder of the milestones I have taken.

I once said 'no one should underestimate the long-term effect of domestic abuse' and I couldn't feel this anymore in this moment of my life.

Do you ever feel like you are in a mental fight when you are trying to overcome something?

Why I Stayed [December 2023]

Recently I recorded a podcast with Alison Bird on why she doesn't leave, it's available to listen to now on the #AbuseTalk Podcast.

I fell upon the hashtag #WhyIStayed and felt called to share the different reasons as to why I didn't leave. I'm sharing them on my Twitter (@JenLGilmour) every morning at 8am over the festive period but I feel it may go beyond that. I'm hoping it highlights the complexities of a relationship that's abusive and shows that it's not just as easy to leave. I started tweeting on Monday so there are already a few up to read.

I have had many comments and heard others speak about the questions they get and the opinions of others, "I would have just left", "I would have hit him back", "I would have left as soon as it started", "Why didn't you leave?". Of course I look back and think the same, why didn't I leave, why did I let it go on for so long and why did I put up with it. But then I remember, it was progressive and he didn't just switch on his abusive behaviour. If it wasn't as simple as reading the ingredients on a tin can, do you think I would have opened that tin can if I had of known?

My debut novel Isolation Junction has the strapline: 100 reasons to leave, 1,000 reasons to stay. I decided on this when I was trying to pre-explain the web of reasons, the cords that tie you down, the way it feels like you have no choice.

Christmas was once a difficult time of the year for me, the bad memories still surface as I come towards the time of the year. I know that there will be many feeling scared, worried and living in fear. That's why I want to share with everyone why I stayed.

Running from my past [September 2021]

I decided to delve into the Couch25K programme and it's taken me more than 9 weeks to complete it. The reason why I started was that I wanted to challenge myself to achieve a goal with exercise without focusing on just the weight loss.

When I was in High School I used to be the person that came second in all the sprints and cross country, there was a girl I could never beat. Naturally, when I left school all of my active side of life came to a slow halt.

2021 has been about putting myself first, putting my oxygen mask on to be able to be the best I can be for my work and my family. It's the first time I've ever put myself first without feeling guilty and it's easier to do because I know this is an investment that will pay off.

I started the programme feeling like weeks 1, 2 and 3 were a breeze. I didn't feel challenged at all, I was enjoying it thoroughly and wanted to do more. I started week 4 feeling ready to go but toward the end of the week I felt I had hit a wall, I ended up having to repeat this week. Week 5 was very similar but there was a significance to this week and I needed to move past it. If you haven't done the programme before, the last run of week 5 is the biggest step up and you've just got to put your head into gear and get through it.

I wasn't going to give in, I had started sharing my journey on social media. I was lucky enough to have a couple of people motivating me to push through this area and reassuring me it was normal, it would become easier after this big leap.

The day arrived for me to get this run done so I could move onto week 6, I set off as usual and around halfway through I was suddenly transported back in time. I was in the early parts of my relationship with my ex and he was chasing me down the road, this had followed an argument over something minor and it was the middle of the night. I remember feeling scared, my heart rushing and not having enough breath. I did suffer from exercise-induced asthma and I could feel that chest tightening. I slipped through a cut-through, thinking I was clear of him and sat against the wall trying to gasp for oxygen.

That was it, it wasn't my capability at all, it was the panic of starting to run and for a long period of time. I recognised that before I was meant to start running I would build myself up and start panting, it was subtle enough for me not to think on it.

That day I failed at that particular run but I knew I needed to go away and work out what was going to help me for the next time. I didn't want him to win, in fact, it made it even more desirable for me to complete this run.

Weeks later and I am on week 9, I tell the world that I am going to smash it on a set day and guess what… I DIDN'T!

It took me three attempts to complete the last run and officially graduate from the programme.

I wondered why I couldn't do it for that final run…

was it because I hadn't resolved the memories in my head

was it because I knew that I would accomplish something

was it a potential trauma bond

was it because I was simply making excuses

Whatever it is, I know one thing was certain, it felt like I was running from my past physically.

Empowering Change for Unplanned Interviews with Children [October 2023]

Going back almost a decade, there was no law in place to support me as someone who had experienced a coercive controlling relationship for several years. I did however receive the local support of Hull Domestic Abuse Partnership and had my very own support worker, without this support I wouldn't have moved forward with my life as much as I have done.

There was an experience within my journey in which I was pulled into an interview with the police, I assumed the meeting was to deliver a response to the first interview and to deliver the CPS decision. This wasn't the case at all, I travelled 30 miles to a location, it was within the lockdown, there was a detective and a police officer to accompany me on this meeting. Once I discovered exactly why I was there, I was immediately triggered and I was instantly started re living what I had suffered, I was dissociating, shaking, couldn't respond and on my own. I didn't have my domestic abuse support worker with me, my partner wasn't with me and the police watched me. Having no idea what to do, they tried talking to me to reassure me I was safe. I didn't know how I was going to drive home, I was feeling sick, I was in and out of reality and there was no need for any of this.

This event stuck with me for weeks and I still remember what it felt like thinking back to it. I can't imagine what it would be like if I were a child were to go through a similar experience.

Nikolai Springfield got in touch with me to explain what had happened to her 6 year old that was interviewed in an unplanned way.

At just 6 years old, our child, who has additional support needs, endured physical and sexual assault at school. But the betrayal didn't end there. The subsequent investigation by police and social work was fraught with negligence, leading to a devastating conclusion: our child was labelled a liar, and the perpetrator faced no repercussions.

Our child is autistic, with pathological demand avoidance (PDA) and attention deficit hyperactivity disorder (ADHD). PDA makes them go to great lengths to avoid demands, even questions. The authorities failed to consider this when conducting their unplanned interview, violating government guidelines.

After nearly two years, we finally received validation from the Police Independent Review Commission: the authorities had not planned the interview appropriately.

We've lost friends and even family support in this battle, but we refuse to stand down. For if they can do this to us, they can do it again, to another innocent child and another shattered family.

A GoFund me page has been set up by Nikolai who wants to take legal action against the authorities that have failed her child. It's needed so that they can pay for solicitor fees, psychological support for her family and to create public awareness initiatives. Empowering change for unplanned interviews with children.

It's not the only way that you can help with Nikolai's cause, you can share her GoFund me or this blog post using #JusticforPJ.

With the success of three kickstarter campaigns I know that crowdfunding can make a difference.

Together we are Louder!Reflection on 'Insight Into My Lived Experiences' [2024]

"Just look at how far you've come"

That used to be something said to me quite often a few years ago and it made me appreciate the life I had in the present at the time.

I remember one of my first speaking events a person asked me a question that threw me off guard at the time,

"Without him you wouldn't have the life you have now, do you think you should thank him?"

I honestly didn't know how to answer this question because my automatic response would be to say no but then I thought about it and I wouldn't have been where I am now without the abuse I suffered. No human being deserves to be treated the way I was, I couldn't live out my basic human rights, the question should be "Why aren't we educated on the warning signs of coercive control in High School or about healthy relationships in Primary School?"

I'm always open to answering questions but some stick with me, some take me back to thinking about the times I should forget. There have been times were family and friends make comments saying "why don't you just move on with your life?" or "It's not healthy for you to relive it or keep talking about what you've been through". But that would mean I would have to ignore my every day struggle, my every day habits that were originally created to protect me, my every day negative thoughts that try and take me down and this would take more energy than it's worth. Looking at this now I see that it's most likely to help them to feel more comfortable, it would be easier to ignore. But the reality is, I'm over a decade on in my life and I'm still working on some of those habits and triggers, there is a long lasting impact and this is what needs awareness as well.

I didn't automatically gain my freedom when I fled and this is the misunderstanding of many, remove the problem and it goes away.

If we look at a physical trauma like a laceration, that laceration will need cleaning, potentially stitches, bandaging up, a course of antibiotics, rest, rehabilitation and even then we see a scar. The scar takes time to fade but it will always remain. Just because it hasn't been a physical trauma doesn't mean we should just ignore it just like we can't ignore an injury.

This is hard for those who haven't been through lived experiences to understand but if you ask someone to name something they had been called that wasn't very nice in the past. You will find that not many people take long to answer, they can name what was said, the person and go on to say that it has affected their self esteem in some way.

This is how we can gain some understanding of how it affects us for a long time.

I often think about the quote I used as part of the introduction to my second book Clipped Wings:

Our wings were clipped, our restrictions were made, our boundaries were tested but now we are free, aren't we?

We look above in the sky at the birds and hope to be free. But the birds make their nests in the trees high above, to protect themselves from predators. Free birds must keep looking over their shoulders the same way all of us have to.'

So, why am I sharing this?

Because despite it being eleven years on for me, I have struggled to read through the lived experiences shared within this first chapter. Despite the number of hours, days, weeks, months and years that have passed I can still remember the emotion I was going through when writing those pieces or the reason as to why it has been written altogether. I've felt that there have been many restrictions that have prevented me from sharing elements of my journey so the parts I have been able to share have usually been carefully assessed, sometimes seeking some guidance on the wording.

Healing is not linear and I have to often remind myself of this.

Lived experiences are powerful and are often the element of learning we miss through text books which is why case studies and human libraries exist.

To those questions and comments about holding on or not moving on I can now reply; I have moved on, I'm using my experiences to help the thousands of people who are in situations like I was; sometimes it may be difficult but I am aware of my mental health and put things into place to help myself. Your support would be most welcome because I need reminding that I am not in that space, the space that can be moved on from but not forgotten.

Reflecting

Domestic Abuse: The never ending jigsaw [October 2017]

After all these years, I still often look back and wonder why it took me so long to realise that something wasn't right. I clearly remember the triggers and the signs but somehow in that moment it wasn't clear how they fitted together.

I look back and I ask myself, 'how could you know which the important events were and how they would fit together?' Years later I'm still piecing together these events like a never ending jigsaw. Events, like jigsaw pieces, scattered in time and place. Really these are the memories that you realise are all part of that bigger picture which makes up abuse. At the time I tried to make the events fit together by altering them just enough for them to make sense but in that format they didn't fit together. Only when I looked at them honestly, objectively and holistically did they make a whole and then I could see the picture that they made. Just like a jigsaw - each piece stands alone until placed together when an entirely different picture appears.

I, perhaps like you, didn't see what each individual episode or event meant and perhaps that is why I allowed the abuse to continue for so long. That is why it happened to me! I sometimes wonder when I will finish this jigsaw or whether I will ever finish it because there are hundreds of realisations, hundreds of signs and a thousand reasons as to why I didn't leave that unhealthy relationship?

Looking back I wonder if I knew what I did now would I try to piece this jigsaw together and look at the bigger picture? Or would it still result in the same outcome?

Even now I'm still surprised, still shocked and still think to myself, How could somebody do that to another human being? How can you isolate somebody? Make them fear you? Threaten them, degrade them, humiliate them, financially ruin them, be violent towards them, turn others against them, make them question their sanity, violate their personal space? How can you put another human being through that? But the sad reality is that some people do all that, and more!

I may never fit all these pieces together and see the entire picture and understand why I went through what I did. But I can now see that the problem never lay with me and I can be reassured that if I had done something differently it still wouldn't have changed the outcome.

However, knowing the warning signs of an abusive relationship may enable others to recognise the signs, the pieces of the jigsaw earlier.

Be aware if this person:

Isolates you from friends and family

Threatens to hurt you or people close to you if you leave

Monitors your movements

Criticises you and constantly blames you for the abuse

Forces you to have sex with them

Controls your life: money, who you see, what you wear

Changes mood suddenly from 'charmer' to 'Hammersley'

Humiliates you in front of others

Says you're useless and couldn't cope without them

Intimidates you into doing what they want

Makes you change your behaviour to avoid making them angry

You can also read case studies to illustrate some of the different aspects of abuse in my newly published anthology 'Clipped Wings: Hear some stories of survival' where you will get a snapshot into the life of a victim. You can find out more about this at;

Surviving is hard [November 2017]

I often think that being a 'survivor' to some extent defines me more than some of the other more positive areas of my life. Ultimately, I think that it is because it's an everyday struggle to overcome its effects despite the years that have passed by.

Many people have wondered why on earth I haven't got over it by now. Well, in answer to that I would say that I have moved on from the person and the act with the exception of a few episodes of frustration. However, the truth is that emotional abuse has a long lasting, residual effect on its 'survivors'.

Does that mean that I am not really a 'survivor'? Does that mean that I'm not over it? Does that mean I'm damaged? Does that mean I am forever trapped?

In answer to that, I would say I am a 'survivor' because I got out and am living a happy and productive life, but I am surviving the daily battle from the emotional scars left behind. I am over it to some extent and have to accept that a part of me was damaged but I am working on me through personal development and that sets me free from the mental entrapment of emotional abuse. I don't think it will ever completely go away because you can't wipe a memory but you can decide whether to let this rule your life or whether to take control and become the person you want to be.

It's not easy being a 'survivor' and no one should underestimate its long-term effect. The dictionary definition of the word 'survivor' is "a person who copes well with difficulties in their life" and this epitomises my belief that however difficult, surviving is worth it on so many levels! Putting my daily struggles aside and looking at my life now, I feel so lucky and some of that stems from an appreciation of what I have now. After the abusive relationship I slowly learnt what happiness felt like, what it felt to be cared for and loved for myself by someone else and finally and most importantly what it was like to love myself and have pride in my own identity.

Looking back on events after the relationship had ended I realised that others need to be educated about this unacceptable behaviour and be able to see what an unhealthy relationship can look like. Many don't realise until it is too late and by then it is accepted that it is normal as it has become a way of life. I can't explain how it works but it needs to be stopped or at least people need to know that it isn't normal at all!!!

I am one who believes in recording things and it has helped me to record my emotions. At first there were so many struggles and I used my desire to help others to write as a channel for my emotions and difficulties and thus my debut fictional novel was born (called " ".) It helped me on so many levels but there were times I couldn't write because I felt so close to it that it was damaging emotionally, I really had to be in the 'right zone'. Now my debut novel is released (and it is a novel rather than a personal account) it feels a little strange. The focus of conversation now is about the message contained within the book and this is an important message to bring hope to many. I feel like I don't have to be quiet anymore, like so many do, about admitting what I went through and through my novel I have been able to share some of the more common behaviours experienced by those affected by emotional abuse and coercive control.

I have been wanting to tell you for a while and to be honest it's only just got to the point where I want to pop it all down and confess. This weekend I have been away to visit family and I have hardly had any time to spend on social media. The times I have I have noticed my author friends posting a pic of their books, letting me know it's a good read for the summer or different ways to read their books. Me... I posted some personal images which was nice. Enjoying the weekend and I notice I hardly ever post about buying my books, a photo of my books, any marketing images. I realised that this was because of my own fears and anxieties. I don't really know why I don't but perhaps it's that I don't want to over post selling posts. So I confess to this and I'm working on it. I guess I have to because the awareness around them is important as well, getting the balance.

Another confession. I feel like a fraud even when I know I'm not. If you haven't seen the TED talk by Amy Cuddy then I suggest you do because I ultimately felt like this in some situations especially when I speak to those in the sector. I don't have a fancy title and I put myself down. BUT HANG ON! I have a wealth of experience and I have had training, I have self learnt a lot, I have spoken with professionals I've worked with as well as the local authority and local MP. I'm not a fraud but I still feel like it and that's the difference.

I spoke to someone about this and they said to me; perhaps the most of us always feel like a fraud because we always strive to the next best thing or the better version of us? Therefore you are succeeding because you feel like this. Food for thought.

I also have another confession. I'm a human being, I'm not a robot and I have emotions. Perhaps sometimes I may seem strong but I have a soft centre. This isn't a bad thing though right? This is good! Because it means I can empathise with others and I care. My job is about helping others and I've always done it… Recently my husband pointed out what I've always done. Helped people. Through my voluntary work, my gap year, my youth work, my job roles, BizMums and what I'm doing now. In fact he pointed out that perhaps that's what I saw in my ex abuser, that in fact I simply wanted to help but I couldn't.

All my confessions here today show a glimpse into the real me and I think the blog cover photo of the iceberg is accurate. I hope you will join in and motivate and encourage me because this is what keeps me strong and going. One day I will know that I can depend on my own confidence but until I have reached that level I know my family, friend, street teamers and more are rooting for me. For that I thank you.

In May I am going to attempt to make more of an effort to share my books on social media. I'm going to work on my confidence and I'm going to work on how to start feeling like I belong. So keep an eye out and feel free to give me a kick up the bum if you don't see it.

NOTE; I discovered my confidence issue at The Happiness Club Retreat and lately I have become more observant of my life to see how it effects me. I can see it is a huge challenge I have to overcome but recognising is the first step.

Thank you for reading and if you feel like confessing, then do so! I confess a lot through #AuthorConfession via Twitter.

Reflecting [February 2020]

Toward the end of last year, I was traveling back from Devon and I had an unexpected conversation with the taxi driver on the way to the train station. I had a pleasant chat with the driver, the usual small talk that you would expect. I seem to intrigue others when they find out about what I do. This time was a little different though because the gentleman told me how his wife had experienced an abusive relationship, he told me about the events that had happened and how he couldn't believe how she was treated. He told me that she is such a loving and caring person and questioned why anyone would do that to her? He told me how they hardly argue and that they work together. It was refreshing to hear about the support he had given her.

I told him about my husband and how he has supported me and how I know what a healthy relationship is like now. I shared the other side though, how looking back I felt for Rob (my husband), in those first months and even years that he 'put up' with me. My anxiety and paranoia of what he may do to me, that I felt the relationship was suddenly going to turn and my trust will be broken again. I spoke about how Rob had stuck by me but questioned where was his support as a new partner to someone who had experienced such trauma? Rob also felt isolated on the path to be by my side, most of the time he made it up and took each day as it came. I know there were times he couldn't understand me and my thought process, I think this is where he would have had benefitted from having some support himself; even if it was to talk through his difficulties.

It really got me thinking about the last six years of my life and the journey I have been on, a lot of people may see my experiences as an individual journey but it hasn't been that at all. Rob has been there to hold me up in the beginning, to holding my hand and finally letting go. It has all been a process and it has taken years to get where I am today. Saying that, I still reach out for him to hold my hand and on the odd occasion he holds me up. I feel very lucky to have had him enter my life and have his love unconditionally.

We created methods to be able to move forward but in the early days he used to constantly refer to two quotes...

"Even the word hopeless has the word hope in it"

"You have to go through the hard times to know what the good times feel like"

I know, it's all well enough saying quotes like this over and over again... but he was right and I can see it now. I can use them when I am feeling rocky on my journey or something comes back to bite me. I know I will get through it and I think about these two quotes that he used to repeat to me.

Thinking about it made me think about what a strong person he is and how he has adopted this into his life. I wanted to be able to do this for myself and have this outlook on life. In return I know there have been moments in which I have been able to remind him.

My husband and that taxi driver aren't the only good people out there, it has taken me a while to recognise that I don't need my defense system on ultra-sensitive all the time.

Trapped [April 2022]

The following is a piece I wrote when I suffered a CPTSD episode as I woke up in the middle of the night.

I didn't realise that I was going to feel restricted.

I didn't realise that I was going to remember the moments.

The memories of feeling like there was no way out.

No way out. No where to go.

My breathing starts to suffer as I need to gasp for air.

It's ok. I'm in control. I'm not there.

I try to convince myself that these are just the flashes of thoughts, they will pass, I am no longer in that place.

The place that pulls me down, that makes me scream internally.

The place that is not just one but many.

I didn't deserve to be stuck, to be frozen, to have no way out.

I take some deep breaths. I take a pace around the room to cool down. Have a glass of water.

Things feel calm but then other memories flash up before my eyes. I'm back in all the places I've ever felt trapped.

Forever trapped by the invisible prison I've been put in.

Deceit [May 2022]

I cannot explain what has happened over the last few months but this sums up how I am feeling now when I reflect on everything. Writing is once again playing an important role in my life, it's my own therapy.

Deceit

I think back and I can see clearer

I can see the false words of support

The selfish game in your movements

Patronising comments that were taken as helpful remarks at the time

My loyalty and trust deserved your respect alone

The missing pieces of the jigsaw have been discovered

The deceit, the betrayal and the cover ups

At least I'm grounded knowing I made the right steps and now make the right choices

There's no more people pleasing, there's no more of you having pressured expectations on me, there is no more friendship

I will find peace and will find calm because I know what I deserve

I will accept nothing less

I will be free to make my own choices, be liberated and empowered

I will be me.

My experience of dating colleagues in the past [January 2024]

First relationship 20-25

Second relationship 25-33

Dating colleagues in my workplace has been a complete fail for me in life and I wish I had recognised why our relationship worked as colleagues/friends and not as partners in the workplace or out of the workplace.

My first experience of dating a colleague at work was when I was only 20 years of age, I was in a job to support my income whilst studying at university. I was working in the local cinema and took advantage of the perks of free films and discount for my uni friends and family members. I discovered that those working in the cinema had the obvious love for films in common so there were so many different conversations in the workplace. The type of person working there was outgoing, fun, likes to be social, had an impressive DVD collection and had banter.

It's clear looking back that banter should stay banter, it's a word that lacks context and is made for as an excuse. But there was one member of staff that had been working there for quite some time, he was the life and soul of the team and would take on any extra shifts. I got on really well with him from the beginning and alongside his humor, pranks and chat- you could talk to him. I didn't find him attractive but I didn't find him unattractive, it was his personality that drew me in. We started seeing each other and at first, things were a win win situation with seeing each other at work and then having that social time, it almost blended the social into work.

Time escalated quickly with this relationship and we were soon moved in together, just because of circumstances. I was thought of quite highly at work and had started to do some administration for them working alongside the supervisors and managers. I was more than happy too but he wasn't really happy because he'd worked there for years and hadn't been given that opportunity. It started to become a problem and it wasn't my fault that the management had recognised my Monika-style skills of organising. A job opening came up for a supervisor role and he was putting his name in for it, the management team asked me to apply for it and I wanted to as it meant more money. He was not happy at all and begged me not to go for it, I decided that I didn't really need to because I was at university so didn't put my name forward. However, he had a pre-interview that stated his sickness rate would mean he was disqualified from the process of application as you need to be dependable. I was approached again to apply for it as there was only one other application. I was put in a position where half of me wanted to go ahead and go for it and the other was told that he wouldn't cope with it because I'd be higher than him. At the time I was young and thought I was in love, thought he wanted to be the breadwinner and didn't see the red flags. I didn't go for it and it went to this one other person by default who became a manager less than a year later. It stopped that feeling of being pulled at both ends.

I wish I had known the red flags of an unhealthy relationship back then because in the end I only worked 4-6 hours a week due to his jealousy. I was trapped in a coercive controlling relationship that meant I stopped studying at university after receiving a Diploma and was financially in trouble.

On hindsight, we should have remained friends and left banter for what it was, banter. I believe our personalities would have worked better this way. I felt for the managers at the workplace as they were put in an awkward position at times but I am thankful that they could see the big picture.

I should have learned from this experience but when we separated I decided to get a part-time job so that I could financially support myself and the two children I had with him. I had a love for gaming and so I applied for a stress free retail job at Game, I just needed something easy and distracting from the turmoil I was going through.

In preparation for this job I decided to privatise all social media and try to find my identity as a person, not just a mum of two living on a council estate. I was embarrassed about the separation from my husband and that I would be a divorcee just like my parents. I was only 25 and so I felt like I needed to live that part of me out in work, it did just that, it was a mental respite. That was until things got extremely stressful with my ex and I started to enter work and throw up before my shifts, I was hardly eating and losing weight fast. I lost 3 stone within two months.

My manager noticed that I wasn't well and one day called me in for a chat, he told me he had recognised my sickness / weight loss / lack of sleep / change in mood. I broke down and told him everything, that I have two children, what was going on with my ex and how things were for me. He simply listened and put into place support at work including concerns over childcare, it took the pressure off me a little. We became friends as through the weeks ahead and I learned that he was unhappy, he was working late into the night as most managers back then were given a lot of responsibility for very little. I offered to help because he had helped and we were soon flirting and started to see each other.

It caused problems at work when we were found out by one of his main supervisors and it put her in an awkward position. He ended up being suspended when it had leaked out from someone seeing us in public together. I don't regret how things went for us, he is a kind man and helped me greatly in such a troubling time of my life. I ended up being with him for almost 9 years, married, had a child together, was living our best lives at the time. Covid hit and it changed everything for us, looking back I could see we had more of a friendship / team relationship more than a romantic relationship. But I hadn't learned or hadn't done that dating thing right. He would have made a great friend but wasn't the right partner. In 2023 our divorce came through, we still talk and get on but I don't think we can have a friendship like we did when we worked together.

As a result, I am a two times divorcee with three children, I wouldn't change my children for the world but It has taken a lot of energy to overcome these experiences. I now work to educate others on healthy relationships, spotting the pink flags before the red flags are present and you're in too deep.

It's not the same for everyone but I think we have to remember that our work colleagues see a different version of us at work, almost like the good-behaved version. Of course, we are appealing to our colleagues because they haven't experienced all the elements of what makes a person a person. Social events are the same, some of your personality slips but it's fun to learn about a person. Work colleagues are exactly that, they are seasonal friends, but do they make good relationships? In my opinion, no, you see the shop window of a person and don't see the prices on the tags inside.

Reflection on 'Reflecting' [2024]

Reflecting on my reflections is certainly comical in my mind. But what I have learned from looking back through these reflections is something I'm most proud of and it almost had to be pointed out to me by my therapist last year.

I have mastered the ability to work hard to understand my past and why it has an impact on my emotional reaction to this day. Without looking back at the trauma and brushing it under the carpet, it's ignored and will come up in almost an uncontrollable way at the most difficult times.

However, this isn't me telling you I've 100% fixed myself or someone can use a formula and you're good to go, I do apologise. I have to work on my regulation to my emotional reaction so that I can activate the logic side of my brain instead of the feeling side of my brain. It's also to note that it's not just the relationship that was abusive that makes an imprint on your feelings. Personally, I have CPTSD so I have to fight my reaction hard at times. I often find that my reaction is heavier when I'm not focused which costs a significant amount of energy, it gets easier with time but it can still creep in and usually it's when I'm past tired and overwhelmed all rolled up into one.

A friend once described it to me as; Imagine an old TV set that requires and aerial to be tuned in, when you are focussed you are like a good signal with clear image and the sound working. Sometimes the aerial gets knocked which means the picture isn't as clear and the sound is distant with snowy static over it, you are able to tune it back in but it takes a little work. Then there are other times that take you out of the blue and everything shuts off, all the tuning of the channels is lost and you get a complete snowy screen and deafening static noise, this is because the TV is set to be tuned that way in the beginning. Tuning the channels could take a lot of work, finding the instruction manual, disagreements between those using it on how to resolve it, missed TV episodes come to frustrate you and you may end up sitting in a bothered state asking why it doesn't work. Your factory settings have been changed to adapt to the environment you were living in, when you are tuned in (which costs energy) you will run through your life with knocks that just need some adjustments but a trigger will knock you back to your factory settings and it's much harder to tune back. You need to work on those factory settings, be kind to yourself, allow time out, look at self care whilst you are able to work out how to tune back in.

It's taken some time but because I'm good at self reflection I am able to identify what would have helped me at that time, what I need if someone else is there with me, what could be done to make me feel safe and how to prevent another incident in the future. I've started to learn the instruction manual and not have to reference it to tune myself back in to the right channels.

It doesn't help when you are in the moment sometimes, a new trigger seems to surface and knock you off your feet or you learn about a new channel that isn't 100% clear picture (Channel 5 for us in the UK).

Are your channels tuned? Do they regularly reset to factory (survival) settings? What channels need your focus?

Recovery And Healing

Biting my nails [February 2018]

I never bite my nails but what I really mean is that I am on the edge of my seat, scratching an itch, twiddling my thumbs.

I simply have the urge to write and get the words, sentences, plot, story and thoughts out of my head and onto paper. For the last few weeks it has been waking me up at night, bugging me in the day, distracting me. I have a note on my iPhone with typed up bits and pieces but I know it's not good enough, I keep telling myself that I need to spend an hour to put my mind at rest. An hour should be easy right? I should be able to fit that in? I'm sure you are thinking the same as me- what's the problem?

When I was unwell this played with my focus a lot, especially when on certain medications. I am exhausted and end up falling to sleep at my desk. However I am proud that I have managed to start a spider graph and trying to do it little by little.

My idea, funnily enough isn't related to domestic abuse and this is a delight because it's given me some free space to enjoy. It's important to take breaks and be disciplined to know if it's personally damaging.

Don't worry though because I have planned also to write a short story in relation to domestic abuse.

Clearing out old memories [February 2018]

I stumbled upon a day in which I decided it needed to be done, I needed to get rid of the last slices of bad memories. I had a few items of clothing hanging up in my wardrobe and a casual dress I would wear every summer to lounge around in. I was actually quite fond of the clothes but I couldn't keep them any longer because of what I carried around with me when I wore them.

I was sad to throw away the dress but not the items collecting dust in the wardrobe. When I say throw away I mean I took them to a clothes bank, although I did wonder for a moment if I should just put them in the bin because of the negativity I feel lives in them. The only reason I had kept a hold of them was because when the toxic relationship had come to an end I was in I was left financially ruined and with only a few bags to call my own; I had no money to invest in the clean slate that I truly wanted. Its taken years to finally wash the slate clean and it really has brought me karma even if it was just that these particular items of clothing are no longer in my home.

Every time I put this nice lounge about dress on it brought that feeling of,,, I wore this when I was with him and it followed onto the dark memories all surrounding my appearance; "that top is too low" "you have more roll backs then Asda" "are you trying to look like a prossy" and it goes on. Those years I began to hate the reflection in the mirror and I put on weight, I could never loose it like he pressured me to. Why would I want reminding of this? Why didn't I let go sooner? It had taken years to slowly change my wardrobe but I didn't throw these out until now. I can't say why and I didn't intend on it but I do know that I should have done this sooner. You can never completely have a clean slate but I have cleaned it the best I can.

I've taken away most of those triggers and I feel like a huge weight has been lifted off my shoulders. I wonder how many others have gone through this, have felt those reminders, have held onto them and for what reasons. I do know that whatever gives you a healthier mindset to pursue it if it helps. I have spent the last several years rebuilding my life and I guess some may call this rehabilitation.

I don't need to visit Isolation Junction again but the truth is you still can and in ways that I wouldn't have thought, through nightmares, flashbacks, triggers in everyday life. They will reduce in time but its finding ways to help reduce them, help them fade away as much as they can.

My meaningful purchase [February 2018]

It was rare for me to buy something for myself, especially without that feeling of guilt. But when I made this purchase for myself there were a lot of final feelings. I will explain of course...

I have had a rush of what freedom feels like once again, this particular moment it overcame me. In fact I was in shock for a while, I didn't know whether to cry or whether to smile; so I nervously laughed whilst I figured out my own emotions.

When you invest all your time into fighting for what you believe in and it finally gets actioned … it's almost seeing what the end looks like. The end could be anything for anyone, it could be the end of fighting and illness, the end of a family feud, the end of a financial strain, I'm sure you understand what I am trying point out here.

When you come to the end, you wonder what are you going to do with all that time you spent investing on fighting for the end? And that's what happened to me and in an unexpected way.

After a day of it sinking in, I realised all I had to do was smile. That what I was feeling was in fact that sense of freedom I have yearned for and I don't need to be afraid of it. It's something we all deserve and should have. I understand what freedom is about and I know others are with me – check out this blog post on what does freedom mean to you?

So… to make this feel official I had to add to my pandora charm bracelet. I had to mark it with another charm because each one of my charms has a story behind why it has a place on my wrist.

Side one has the word Free engraved.

Side two has this inscription *'Sometimes you've gotta fall before you fly'*

I am sure you can see why I bought this charm to add to my collection.

Let me know if you have a bracelet with charms that mean something to you.

Starting my day with a smile [March 2018]

I was delighted to have spent a weekend at The Happiness Club retreat. I originally wanted to go on this retreat to be able to create an addition to the support I give to victims, survivors and those in the sector of domestic abuse. Also to go for myself as I believed it would help me grow as a person and enable me to take the steps I need to take to move forward in my journey and not be held back by my own feelings and fears. Yes I have fears, I am human (saying this with a smile and a wink).

I am not very good at giving myself time out and relaxing, those that know me know that I am always on the go and busy. I speak with victims and survivors at all hours of the day and I fit in writing, social media, my blog and around this. Not to mention my family life.

I was so excited to hear that I had received part funding to be able to invest back into myself.

The retreat was at Shringley Hall in Macclesfield, a 4* Hotel and spa, I loved spending time in the spa which was in the church building you can see on the photo above. The weekend was perfect as today is in fact my 30th birthday so we had some celebratory drinks as well.

I am going to be odd here and tell you about the last exercises we did. We paired up and for a whole two minutes you had to say as much positive attributes about the other person, they had to write them down and then we swapped over. These in turn would become your daily affirmations to say to yourself each day.

I was lucky enough to have Jo Howarth herself and this is what she said about me:

Inspirational

Caring

Loving

Open and honest which shows that I am courageous

Inteligent

I know my aim and where I am going

Encouraging

Give people a voice

The funny thing is that in another exercise we did (which involved visualising the best version of yourself) this is what I wanted to become. I hadn't ever thought that this might have already come across. It felt rather strange but nice at the same time.

What would your affirmations be?

This is me! [June 2018]

Every time I hear or watch this song from The Greatest Showman I have this burn inside to break free and let everyone see what being me is really like. One day I know I will be able to share more but for now I share glimmers through my blog posts and share all.

I want to share why the song resounds with me and which parts really stand out and give me that burning feeling, each time I listen to it I find myself quite emotional as I am sure many others can relate for different reasons.

Here's the song which you can listen/watch now…

I'm not a stranger to the dark, hide away they say, cause we don't want your broken parts. I've learned to be ashamed of all my scars.

Straight away I am hooked on the first line, it's true, I feel I am not a stranger to the dark. The feeling of being alone, hiding away and being broken. Many years I spent hidden, only few knew some of what was happening behind closed doors and my ability to mask the truth to protect him and my own embarrassment and shame was what I felt my only option to pretend to lead a 'normal' life. Even now I can find myself feeling shameful of what I went through, my scars that cut deep and struggle to heal. BUT the more I open up to the truth the more people know who I am and why I do what I do now.

When the sharpest words want to cut me down, I'm gonna send a flood, gonna drown em out.

This reminded me a bit about the one song that I depended on to keep me going and one that is referenced in Isolation Junction, Skyscraper. I hope that by what I am doing now I send a flood and drown the hurtful things that were once said to me. I recently shared a blog post on what he used to call me and I was surprised to the response, people relating, offering compliments to build my confidence, offering a reason as to why this may have been said.

I am brave, I am bruised, I am who I'm meant to be... THIS IS ME.

I didn't used to be brave, in fact I can wobble at times. There were days that I faked my courage and faked my bravery to make a difference to others. Thats ok though, because I needed to be able to feel a sense of bravery and courage even if it wasn't all there, I needed to know I could do it and carry on. If I hadn't I would have crumbled before now and wouldn't be where I am today.

I'm not scared to be seen, I make no apologies... THIS IS ME.

Again originally I was scared, I was scared on how my message was going to be taken but now I can say I am not scared to speak out about what needs to be done, what I went through and if it helps others then I have done my job. It has become a passion, a drive and I have found my direction in life. I won't apologise or stop helping others because the world needs people like me, like the connections I have, people learn and understand from our experiences, get help, relate and more.

Another round of bullets hits my skin, well fire away, they say, I won't let this shame sink in.

Believe it or not, I still get fired at, and back when I started this project the bullets hit my skin and they did sink in and hurt. I am able to switch off from anything like this. There are still aspects I haven't overcome in my past yet but I know I am doing my best and I am determined that I can continue my path to lead a happy life and to the full, I deserve to be free.

We are warriors!

For all victims and survivors. We stand together and we warrior through our days to get to the end, together we are stronger and louder. Our network of brave warriors will keep each other standing up, keep each other going, get through the bad days, encourage and motivate, understand and be brave. We are united. We are not alone. You are not alone.

Lyrics in italics from The Greatest Showman.

Together we are Louder [September 2018]

For a while I have used a few different slogans and created my own quotes. A few weeks ago I asked my street teamers to help me finalise one I wanted to voice at the end of my YouTube videos. Something that was going to knit everything together and share what I am working on and towards. I had a few in mind and with some feedback, tweaking was done and it was decided.

'Together we are louder'

And to introduce the slogan, what better way then a video uploaded to the world with me wearing a bright red top and the slogan in big letters.

What quotes and slogans impact your life?

Dreams and nightmares [January 2019]

Ever since I can remember I have been a heavy sleeper, my dreams and nightmares can feel very real. I used to think everyone was like this but as

I grew older I found that it was more unusual than usual. I could sleep walk, have conversations, scream in fear, show other emotions and more. I've learnt that the more stressed I am the more I respond in my sleep, I am hoping this makes sense.

I had a dream the other night and it had a combination of factors but one aspect was that my husband slept with someone else. Now I know my husband and we are in this amazing loving relationship and I can clearly say this would be completely out of character, he just wouldn't do it. I know I had a conversations earlier that day and it triggered old memories with my ex abuser. I know that this had a part to play with my subconscious and it came to shake me in my sleep. I told my husband all about it the next day, it's hard because the dreams for me are very real and I feel the emotions that I experienced in my dream. When I say real, I mean I can remember what people were wearing, what setting it was in, where I would walk, what I would see, like I am actually there- until I wake up.

It reminded me of the dreams and nightmares I had within that old relationship and also within my recovery. To give you an idea: In the relationship I would have dreams of escaping in all different kinds of ways, old boyfriends or family and friends would appear to help me. I would wake up and see my ex abuser next to me and start to sob, I wanted to go back to sleep, I wanted it to be real. I would have nightmares of aliens or demons coming to get me in my sleep, I would wake up and see the room with those characters in it but I couldn't move; it was as if I was paralysed. Sleep was never a good time for me because I could be disturbed in my sleep in the most horrible ways or I would have these night terrors. I often woke up shivering in the wet sheets that was my sweat.

Now my husband can tell how I am doing by what I am like in my sleep. When things were 'fresh' from the flee I was a very disturbed sleeper, crying out loud, screaming, rolling about, arguing and whimpering. Sometimes I wouldn't remember the dream or nightmare and sometimes I would, it was a very unsettling time. As time has moved on the calmer my sleep has been and now there seems to be only snoring I hear about from my husband, yes I am a snorer. Like I mentioned in the beginning, if something comes up that triggers memories then it will influence my sleep and my husband will know if I am not doing as well as usual.

My dreams have slowly changed over the years and I am glad to have more happy dreams that make me feel I can get through the day rather then hinder it.

I wonder if anyone will relate to this?

How grounding helps with my triggers [July 2021]

Have you ever had one of those moments where you just take in the world? You think wow, it's so beautiful, I'm just a tiny part of it. Well I've had a few of those moments and I want to seek them out more.

My first moment was my first time on an aeroplane when I was around 12/13 years old. I remember going into the cockpit with the pilot and seeing the blanket of clouds around me. I feel lucky to have had that experience as a child because it was magical.

The second was when I was 18 and went gorge walking in the Yorkshire Dales. It was breath taking walking through the crack of the earth and looking up at the sky. Gorge walking is about squeezing your way up a gorge by climbing, rock hopping and jumping in water. It was very surreal and felt like I was as small as an ant might, it's an experience I need to repeat.

Those moments are imprinted in my mind and I know the next ones are waiting for me when I go travelling some day. But for now I take in what's around me, when I see a field of blooming wild flowers I see the colour and clearly the invitation to capture it. I recognise these moments can also be in awe of historical buildings, architect and events.

To me these moments are important because they ground me, it reminds me that I'm a part of something much bigger. It also means that the memories I have held onto that happened before the abusive relationship I experienced haven't been forgotten, my past experiences are not a waste.

The purpose of grounding techniques is to allow you to step away from negative thoughts or flashbacks. It can decrease the intensity of your feelings by distracting them using the five senses.

When I have a trigger or when I'm going through a low point this is what helps me. These moments aren't always available when I'm in need of them so I seek them out wherever I am. I go outside and look at the green in the flowers, I soak in the sky and listen to the birds. I breathe and think I am no longer with him, it's ok, I am here now and you can get through this.

Don't get me wrong, this has taken years and at first it wouldn't have worked. But this is where I am now, it's almost like taking me out for a reality check because I certainly don't want to feel as if I'm back there in that situation. I have been able to take these steps forward because of The Recovery Toolkit, that was my starting point to find the tools I needed to help me live my life.

My weekends are spent walking and visiting new places, it offers a mental break from a busy week. It almost feels like a preventative because if I don't go out at the weekend it reflects in the week ahead. It feels like it becomes a natural state of mind and something that isn't as forced but is a part of my subconscious.

Do you use grounding techniques?

When I lay [May 2022]

Finding my sexuality has been a part of my healing journey which has been an extremely challenging time, I spoke very openly and raw about it on the #AbuseTalk Podcast if you want to hear more. But I wrote this one morning when I spent some time reflecting.

When I lay

When I lay staring at the ceiling

When I wonder why I never knew

When I think about the lost time that can never be reclaimed

When my body talks to me

When I finally know the pieces click together

When I feel the contentment embed itself within me

When I lose the worry about other people's opinions and views

When I allow myself acceptance

When I first feel comfortable

When all my questions have been answered

That's when I get to say that I am truly me.

Solo Holiday Healing [July 2022]

I'll soon be doing something I have never done and that's going on a solo holiday. In February I shared a blog post about how I have been working through an identity crisis. I knew back in November that I needed to take space away from everything and everyone but I was unable to do this. That's going to all change as I spend a week in Greece which is going to be filled with taking the space I need but I will of course go on adventures.

When I first left the abusive relationship I was anxious about walking down a street on my own. It took steps to go onto public transport because of my anxiety levels. I remember getting on a train on my own for the first time, I didn't feel comfortable being on my own. This came from being overshadowed by his presence in the relationship and moving on to thinking he knew my whereabouts at all times.

Going on a plane for the first time EVER without another adult is going to be a huge milestone for me. Followed by attempting to have guilt-free time to give my mind a break and actively practice healing.

I know this is going to be an incredible challenge for me but I know deep down that I deserve to take this mental break.

You've probably noticed changes to my content on social media and here on my blog, there's been a lack of consistency and I have been working on being comfortable in my own skin. I know that having the chance to reset will allow me to come back with fresh eyes. I have had to protect myself from further mental strain over the last few months and so I have been careful about how much material I consume that's linked to domestic abuse. Having the ability to do this for me shows that I have grown because there was a time I would have burnt myself out completely.

In the last 9 months of my life:

Diagnosis of a medical condition

Discovered my sexuality

Uncovered unhealed sexual trauma

Realised I was living with the survival tactics I created in the abusive relationship

Identity Crisis

Childhood Trauma surfaced

Separated from my husband

Surviving as a single mum of three and running two businesses

I started this journey of sharing my lived experiences of domestic abuse around five years ago and it only feels fair to share this with you. Some will wonder why I don't keep it personal, my reason is that the world is full of edited feeds and that can be very isolating. I know the different aspects of my journey make a difference and I will continue to share until it stops doing so. I receive emails and messages all the time with expressions of how my story has helped. Perhaps I am sharing this because recently I have felt vulnerable.

Behind the scenes, I have been finalising my latest project The Funky Frecks in the hope for it to be published in September. I have also been journaling heavily about what I am learning about myself and I am sure this will be material that can be shared in the future when I feel more comfortable.

Thank you for your continued support and I look forward to sharing just how much my solo holiday helps me in my healing journey.

Losing Time [August 2022]

I made it back from my solo holiday and I managed to write a few pieces whilst I was away. Going away was all about taking a step forward and recognising my healing process, you can read more in the blog post Solo Holiday Healing. I want to share with you this piece which I wrote when I was transfixed on the view and time became irrelevant.

Losing Time

I sit on the beach

I stare out at the sea

I see hills in the distance

I appreciate the glass like water

I enjoy seeing people enjoying each other's company

I hear the crickets chirping

I feel the sun kissing my skin

I taste the salt in the air

I appreciate the clear sky

I look to the furthest point, the edge of the world

I want to be at peace

I search for answers

I question my choices

I challenge my thoughts

I wonder why I've gone through what I have

I fight the numbness to try and feel

I know that I'm here for a reason

I try to be kind to myself

I lift my head a little higher

I quietly thank those who have been there no matter what

Healing is not Linear [October 2023]

Yesterday I started therapy and I am trying to remain hopeful.

I have experienced counselling when I was in an abusive relationship around 11/12 years ago, I went again around 5/6 years ago with a completely different service. I found that it did help but my first experience it was clear it was to do with the relationship which meant my situation needed to change. My second experience I had was limited to 12 sessions, we were able to do a few more than this but even she realised that my trauma was too complex for just listening.

My hope is that this long term therapy will enable me to make my own decisions free of other peoples opinions or past trauma memories interrupting the decision making process. I want to be able to manage my triggers in a healthier way.

I'm sharing this because I haven't exactly been present for the last year and I have been comforted by quite a few concerned people that have followed me on social media. But I didn't accept their help and I didn't want to share with the world that I need to take time for myself because I would see it as a failure.

Yes I am an advocate for women who are or have been abused, yes I raise awareness, yes I signpost, yes I will get involved in campaigns where I can but I am still a survivor myself. I am someone with lived experiences, I am someone who doesn't shy away from that or my healing journey.

In the last year I have also had someone respond negatively on social media because they felt that my message wasn't clear within our communication compared to what was said online years later. I have held onto these comments despite knowing that this is all circumstantial. Whenever I speak with someone I signpost in a voluntary manor and always say I am not a professional, I am someone with lived experiences.

It reminded me of what was once said to me that took some of the weight from my shoulders as a recovering people pleaser, "you only know what you know at that time". When I first published my debut novel Isolation Junction I was in a very different place to where I am now, I've taken the time to learn, to heal, to listen and to be kinder to myself.

If I went back in time to rewrite my story knowing what I know now, of course it would be completely different. If I went back and went through everything again with the brain I had at that time, I would have still made those choices knowing what I knew at that time.

Equipping myself is the only way that I will move forward, a decade has passed since I fled and yet I am here feeling like I am back on day one. That feeling goes quickly when I think back to what day one was like and the strength it has taken to get her, I am on day one but I'm not in the same chapter nor the same book.

Healing is different for everyone

Healing doesn't follow tasks you have to do to achieve completion

Healing for those with trauma is a continuous effort for years and years to come

Healing is not linear

Be patient with yourself as I have tried to be for me.

As a part of this next step in my journey, I have started writing again and I hope to be more present but for now I make no promises. I know what I share will be right for the time I am posting it and I hope it helps you.

October is Domestic Violence Awareness Month and usually I do something to mark the month, this year my energy has to mostly be for me but this does not mean that I am not thinking about it's importance.

Together we are Louder

Trauma Recovery: Physical and Emotional [November 2023]

In 2023, I had three different major surgeries; In January I had a full hysterectomy, in June I had a right ACL reconstruction plus a meniscus disc re-anchored and finally last week I had a left ACL reconstruction. All three have felt very different on my own pain scale but one thing they all have in common is that the time to be "fully recovered" is one year. However, each surgery has a different physio programme to follow. The programmes are a set of different exercises and potential milestones but I was assured that each person is different and milestones will be reached exactly when my body can reach them.

Thankfully I spent a good year becoming the fittest I could possibly be before my first surgery, I lost a lot of weight and toned up. Following my hysterectomy I was then able to do post op physio ready for my planned bilateral ACL reconstruction surgery planned for June. However, the surgery didn't fully go to plan because when they went into my right knee there was a lot more damage to fix hence why I had to go back for my left knee.

But what does this have to do with the trauma recovery I really want to talk about? Trauma from being coercively controlled by my ex husband.

Well, this year I have seen for myself just how long it takes to recover from these individual surgeries. What surprised me was the ACL reconstructions, they didn't seem like the most invasive surgery you could end up with for your knees. But, my legs ended up swelling up and the bruising on my chin and the back of my knee was just as bad as my knee itself. Then there was the ability to put your weight onto your leg after this surgery. I'm sure you are getting the picture.

This has opened my eyes to how much the body can take but also what it needs to do to repair itself, including the energy it takes from you physically. My body has suffered immense trauma this year and I am doing everything in my power to repair it because I know how important it is to me in the long run. It feels like an almost holistic approach, every patient is different, every patient is on their own pain management and physical recovery journey.

Why then did I not consider the amount of time, patience, help, support or guidance needed for emotional trauma? It will be even longer than the physical trauma my body has gone through this year. When I started to think of it like this I started to feel lighter and asked myself why haven't I been kinder to myself?

Upon this conclusion I realised that...

My mind needs its own physio therapy to exercise through the flashbacks, negative automatic thoughts and unhealthy habits.

My heart needs the presence family, friends or connections to help learn to love and trust again.

My soul needs guidance and the tools to be able to open up and be kind to myself.

Everyone is different, one exercise might work for me but for someone else it might not. We talk about a holistic approach but when you see how it works in a physical trauma way, you realise that it's still missing.

Going back to my recovery from the surgeries, post surgery I had phone calls to check up on how I was doing at home, I had appointments to check my wounds and mobility, I had the pain management side and more. Some weeks I had five appointments face to face. Correct me if I am wrong, but as far as I know we don't do this for those who have had an emotional trauma.

Even physical trauma to the body can relapse and so it's important to also remember that healing is not linear with surgery. I can definitely say that I've been doing well with recovery for a couple of weeks and then suddenly I've been over confident and climbed an extra step or walked around a corner faster than I should, it's then put me back a week.

Emotional trauma can come from situations or events we find traumatic and can include how we're affected by our experiences. Everyone has a different trauma response, so you might notice that it effects you quickly or a long time after the event. Being verbally or emotionally abused is one of the most common forms of emotional trauma, it takes many different forms and can go unrecognised for years.

Reflection on 'Recovery And Healing' [2024]

Just when you think you're their at the promised land of "healed" your brain decides to say "you're ready for the next thing", usually something you've popped to the back of your brain to protect yourself. I often say to my brain "give me a break" because there are times when things come to the surface one after another. If you weren't ready then your brain wouldn't unlock this memory/trauma/survival habit to break, this doesn't mean it's any easier.

Healing is a part of personal growth and without it we remain stuck this is why you can forgive but never forget.

Going back through my healing / recovery just shows how much progress I've made, at times it feels like two steps forward and one back but other times it feels like one step forward and two steps back. There's no right or wrong way to heal but even if you don't see progress at the time there will be a moment when you look back and see that that time was just as important and relevant to your story. There is no straight incline on a progress graph to measure where you are. It's taken me time to accept that this is what it feels like and it's okay to go through emotions even if you have felt them over and over again.

A follower of mine shared a song with me toward the beginning stages of sharing my journey online and it has always stuck with me.

Don't be hard on yourself - Jess Glynne

I came here with a broken heart that no one else could see

I drew a smile on my face to paper over me

But wounds heal when tears dry and cracks, they don't show

So don't be so hard on yourself, no

Let's go back to simplicity

I feel like I've been missin' me

Was not who I'm supposed to be

I felt this darkness over me

We all get there eventually

I never knew where I belonged

But I was right and you were wrong

Been tellin' myself all along

Don't be so hard on yourself, no

Learn to forgive, learn to let go

Everyone trips, everyone falls

So don't be so hard on yourself, no

'Cause I'm just tired of marchin' on my own

Kind of frail, I feel it in my bones

Won't let my heart, my heart turn into stone

So don't be so hard on yourself, no

It's everything I need to hear in my past, present and future. I have found it incredibly difficult to give myself compassion, I often forget that what I've experienced isn't of the norm (combined). I can find myself blurting out my journey to the next stranger who starts a conversation with me, their stunned face and lack of knowing how to respond reminds me that their are people living without multiple traumas.

My healing steps forward have given me the ability to open my mind to the traumas I had when I met the person who abused me. I am now able to be aware of myself when a trigger tries to tear me down, a trauma memory won't leave me alone, I forget that my automatic response is from a survival nature and that my body is trying to protect me. I am rewiring what I know to teach my body that I am in control, can make my own decisions and that I can do anything I would like with my life.

"Don't avoid but do overcome" ~ Jennifer Gilmour

Learning Through Self-Education And Courses

The importance of tackling difficult issues like domestic abuse through fiction [2017]

I'm Jennifer Gilmour, a young married mum of 3, an entrepreneur and now a published author. From an early age, I have had a passion for writing and have been gathering ideas and plot lines from my teenage years. A passionate advocate for women in abusive relationships, I have amalgamated and fictionalised other survivors' experiences alongside my own to write my first novel. It details the journey of a young woman from the despair of an emotionally abusive and unhappy marriage to develop the confidence to challenge and change her life and to love again.

Isolation Junction has been a challenging novel to write and I have written it for a few reasons. I have been the victim of abuse myself. I found myself writing down my feelings in a way to get it out. For many years I have kept a diary; it first hit when I was around 15 and Bridget Jones came out - I wanted her diary. I don't have those diaries from my teenage years anymore and I never really read through them. I did however, find it very therapeutic to write my emotions, highs and lows down and this got me through my early teens.

This was a bit harder; I had to keep a record to remember my emotions on the abusive relationship. You can find yourself minimising the abuse and looking on it and thinking it wasn't that bad, but when reading back on my diary snippets I can see that it is important for me to remember. Isolation Junction was by far not an easy write and there were times I couldn't write because it was damaging emotionally, I really had to be in the right zone. Now my debut novel is released it feels a little strange but now the conversation is about the message of the book and this is the important thing. I feel like I don't have to be quiet anymore about admitting what I went through.

People have seen a different side to abuse through my fictional novel. It's something that has been addressed in a text book rather than a novel. The reaction has been that people have learnt about a different type of abuse and what coercive control can look like. It is hard to explain in a text book to fully demonstrate this type of behaviour. I'm pleased that people are being educated through my fictional story.

I quote a few reviews here to give you a bit of an idea:

"This book I was not able to put down"

"A hugely important book!"

"A very gripping and interesting read"

"Thank you Jennifer for highlighting this issue and hopefully inspiring women to break free from emotional abuse"

"A fictional account of an everyday, unacceptable issue"

The novel has opened up a huge discussion of the behaviour and for those who don't understand, it's enlightened them to see what it could be and the progression behind it. My aim is to encourage questions, challenge the current law and the behaviour itself. It has gotten people thinking about their friendship circle and I have been contacted by many saying, "I have passed your book on to my friend because I think they are in this situation…"

As well as educating, it is also an entertaining book as you can see from the reviews. It is not filled with doom and gloom but features romance and some comedic moments.

I hope that the book will raise awareness of this often hidden and unseen behaviour and empower women in abusive relationships to seek help for themselves and find the confidence to change their lives. I also mention at the end of the book a message from myself and I include a helpline as I recognise that there needs to be a link to support from reading the book.

Now the book is out there to buy, the message needs to be talked about and to break the taboo. The book is just the beginning of blocking the road to 'Isolation Junction', I have put myself forward as an passionate advocate for women in abusive relationships.

Life changing training [September 2017]

Last week I attended a conference in London, in fact it was a two day training that would gain a certificate upon completion for a life changing programme.

I better start right at the beginning with how I learned about this training. In fact, I originally went on the programme as a client. The programme is called and it is for those who have experienced domestic abuse and you have to fit the requirements to be able to access it. You may have heard in my interviews that the idea of came when I was on a course with other women that had been abused, this is in fact that course. I couldn't believe that I was getting educated after an abusive relationship about what an unhealthy relationship looks like and so my initial aim was to educate in an entertaining way and bring awareness to abuse, specifically emotional abuse and coercive control. This course has changed my life and I wouldn't be where I am today if it wasn't for this course. I have a lot to be thankful for and did the programme proud.

After was published I planned to write a second novel which is still my work in progress, I wanted to use some of the programme material and this is when I went in search of the person who created . I had no luck on Amazon or Facebook and so I had got in touch with the facilitators of the program at who gave me the name of the wonderful educated lady who designed it, Sue Penna. I again had no luck on Amazon or Facebook and decided to try Twitter one day, she popped up. The conversation started with a tweet from me, I had to get in touch with her and tell her what a difference her programme had made in my life and also to see if I could gain access to the resource personally. After a couple of weeks we had a phone conversation and I explained about my book, my thoughts for the future, the course as well as thanking her for her time and the programme. Sue was fruitful with information and directed me to a couple of resources as well as informing me that I could become a facilitator of the course by going on the specific training of hers. I was delighted to learn about this and that I could meet Sue herself.

Months later and I am on my way to London to attend this valuable training. I didn't know what to expect other than what I had done personally on the programme as a client. I couldn't believe how engaging the training was and I was excited to be a part of it. Surrounding me were volunteers and workers at different levels in the sector and each shared the same excitement to become a facilitator of the programme.

I encourage any workers and volunteers to seek out this training because it is presented in a way that educates and nurtures the attendee's, making sure that the clients are ready to be informed on certain subject matters within the sessions. I should mention at this point that this is a 12 week course to go on as a client.

It became apparent that my result is in fact of the aim of the programme and I wasn't aware of this at all.

The discussions we had over the two days were very interesting and grabbing and one thing shone out from the whole experience and that was that everyone was passionate about their work. I had the opportunity to make some connections and we all shared conversations outside of the conference as well, even after a glass of wine or two. A lot of people remarked at how the training didn't feel like work but it was also enjoyable and the way it was taught was easy to digest as well as participating in exercises.

A lot of notes taken down, a lot more research to be done and connections to follow up with. One of the exercises toward the end of the training was one I had done on the programme, we were all given an envelope that was required to have our name written on it. Our envelopes were then passed to the right and each person in the group wrote a positive about that person on a post it note and placed it in their envelope. It was passed around until the envelopes came back to your own and then it was required to write a positive about yourself.

I read mine on the way home from London and I thought I would share some with you here;

"You are my new hero, thank you for being you. I have learnt so much from you. Also fun loving, open, love, kind, I look forward to reading your book"

"WOW- I am full of admiration- thanks for your wise words + contributions I learned a lot"

"Jennifer I really admire you. You are, strong, capable, kind and warm. x"

"Very inspiring"

"Brave"

These came at the right time for me as well. I really needed to hear some positives and so you can imagine just how thrilled I was, as well as a little emotional.

Of course the highlight for me was to meet and chat with Sue Penna and I am sure we will be talking in the future. Another exercise was that we told the rest of the group what we enjoyed most about the two days. It came to me and I had managed my emotions well up until this point. I simply had to say from my heart a huge thank you to Sue, that it was an honour and that her programme did change my life and I went on… I was ok until I saw that Sue was also getting teary and then the tears flowed. It was a positive thing and tears of happiness because I never expected to even get this far in my journey. I have to mention that it was also Sue's last time in delivering the course personally as she now has the lovely Roxie to train the programme. I will never forget the time Sue has put aside to have important discussions with me.

Is Domestic Abuse Modern Day Slavery? [March 2019]

One day I received an email stating that my talk wouldn't fit into a certain theme because domestic abuse isn't modern day slavery. Previous to this I didn't say it was, but the event recognises different forms of slavery like sex trafficking and uses performing arts within it to get people to think and respond. I celebrate my freedom each year at this event because I felt like a prisoner; I was trapped, isolated and controlled.

I then started to think about the similarities between domestic abuse and modern day slavery and so I thought I would ask my Twitter followers as well as doing a bit of research. I also wanted to be able to respond appropriately.

On the anti-slavery website it states this:

Slavery did not end with abolition in the 19th century. Instead, it changed its forms and continues to harm people in every country in the world.

Whether they are women forced into prostitution, men forced to work in agriculture or construction, children in sweatshops or girls forced to marry older men, their lives are controlled by their exploiters, they no longer have a free choice and they have to do as they're told. They are in slavery.

At this point I was thinking perhaps the glove doesn't sit exactly but if you read on:

Today slavery is less about people literally owning other people – although that still exists – but more about being exploited and completely controlled by someone else, without being able to leave.

This then made me think the glove did in fact fit better than I at first thought.

So is it modern day slavery? Can it be categorised? Is it yes or no? Or is it a grey area and is it situational?

Personally, it made me think about the abusive relationship I was in. I changed my behaviour to adapt to the controlling abuse I endured, I had to complete chores and if I didn't I would be vulnerable to more abuse, if I didn't have sex within a certain time frame than he would have sex with me whilst I was asleep or threaten to go elsewhere. Leaving an abusive relationship is difficult and dangerous and it isn't as simple as just leaving. I felt that there was no escape and there was no help for me, the threats of what he will do if I tried to leave were enough to keep me for years. There were a lot of other factors I haven't even shared yet, one day I will of course. He presented like he owned me, that I was his possession.

But is it modern day slavery?

I would love to hear your thoughts on the question so please do feel free to comment as I don't have a definite answer or opinion, I think its a work in progress.

But can I speak at events about freedom? YES! I was stripped away of my identity and had become a different Jennifer to adapt to the situation I found myself in. I had no control over money, over everyday activities, over what I wore or who I saw? Now that I am free from that relationship, I appreciate life and how I have the freedom to make my own decisions. I feel blessed and have a new life, I have reclaimed who I am as a person.

Here's the original tweet with the results along with some of the replies:

70% yes

30% no

I never thought if it this way. Now, healthy, and sitting on my floor in a sort of shock, yeah. It totally could be…you need to do a round table of sorts…

@kellys_author

Excellent question. My gut feeling is "yes!" Having been trapped for almost 8 years I know the feeling of "there's no way out, no escape". I hesitate to compare it to slavery with all its connotations but on the other hand… Yes.

@AnitaSGera

Absolutely – the intent behind it is so consistent in the cases I know about. Domestic servitude. subservience, being dehumanized, a chattel / prop. All about power & control and domination

@Tranzform

I think that depends on the circumstances really. Coercive control is used but at the end of the day that almost trivialises things as real slavery like sex trafficking etc. and real slavery like sweat shops so I'm a bit on the fence there.

@PoeticJustice23

I guess to a certain degree it is yeah controlling someone to do what you want by way of threats intimidation etc. yes I agree x

@kayleighw851

I answered yes to that and I will tell people why. Because I was also a childbride and I have analysed it deeply . ANYTHING THAT KEEPS SOMEONE UNDER ANOTHERS CONTROL AND IN PAIN = IS . If the other person is controlled without wanting to be so IT IS . Manipulative Slavery

@Infointeract

Why my past experiences aren't a waste [April 2021]

A photo came up in my memories just a few days ago. A production of A Midsummer Night's Dream with my tutors and fellow students. It was way back when I was at Hull College studying Acting.

I shared this story on my profile and felt it should go further, especially as I've received responses from all three of my tutors from the National Diploma.

This is why I didn't waste my past experiences in life.

Whilst I was in college I didn't believe in myself, my mum had instilled in me that I needed a fall back plan because it's unlikely that this career path would work out for me. It wasn't just my mum though, but the school system and others around me.

I applied for a gap year in Youth work and decided not to apply for anything in Acting. I was absolutely gutted when I received some pretty awesome grades from my diploma in Acting. However, I thought to myself that I would carry on with what I had decided and maybe come back to it. I went on to study youth work at the University of Chester. I found myself doing acting within this, being a part of acting groups and I worked with young people with drama.

My life went in a different direction as most know. I fell into an abusive relationship for several years and I felt my life was on hold. I didn't progress in myself or with any kind of career.

However, the last several years of building myself back up after fleeing that abusive relationship has given me an appreciation for life. The last two years have been a big game changer for me and I believe in myself. I've made sure I take advantage of my freedom and really worked on my self development.

I've taken away the negative support in my life, those who said I couldn't make it or achieve it. In anything I have chosen, I have not stuck to a 'normal' job or typical 'career path' that the school system encourages. I'm not saying that those paths are wrong or bad but it simply wasn't right for me. If my creativity had of been encouraged who knows where I would be? If someone had have told me they believed in me, motivated me and backed me- where would I be?

I may not be the actor I wanted to be in my childhood and teens but those experiences have helped me today. Those skills have been put into practice when I speak at events in the UK or happen to appear in the news or on a documentary. They appear in events I host or interviews I facilitate.

That experience wasn't a waste of time because it only made me certain of who I was meant to be.

If I could go back in time and give myself a message it would be "Believe in yourself and surprise those who don't believe you can do it".

I've surprised myself in the last two years and I hope it's turned the heads of those who said I couldn't do it.

I certainly don't have a typical day at work in my self-employment. I'm never bored and there's a different sense of achievement when something works. My hope is that my children see that there are options and that I pass on the message that dreams can be goals.

So my message to you today is, whatever has happened in your life... it's not a waste! It can equip you with what you need to make it happen. Believe in yourself because that's the number one person you need to convince. If you can't do that, I'm waving a flag with your name on it and I will personally cheer you on.

You never know, there may be an opportunity to do some acting in the future and live the dream I had. I have done some odd jobs throughout the last few years and enjoyed every minute.

I received so many nice comments on this long form post which is certainly a blog worthy post. Three of those replies came from those who taught me at Hull College and I felt I should include them here, they moved me to tears.

Peter – I remember you well Jennifer and you were part of a strong year group. You were unsure of your own abilities, but gradually grew in confidence. You had such a passion and cared so much. All the team that taught you then have now left Hull college, but it was a special team and a time we remember fondly that shared their passion. Many of our students don't always go into the Arts, but they do thrive and find their place. I'm so pleased that you have now found yours and proud we were able to be a part of your journey. Everyone who knocks the value of the arts should read your inspirational story, this is why we teach it.

Scott Solway– This is such a wonderful story. Many students come in a little unsure of themselves and their abilities, I'm sure that it's safe to say that you were in this bracket Jenny. But you always had the ability to develop, a big outstanding element of your life was that you cared about others. I think I can say on behalf of all the team that taught you and your year group (who were hugely talented by the way) that whilst it was an acting course, and acting skills and stagecraft were learnt, our sole aim was always to try and make students better, better people and prepared for everyday life in the big wide world, not just the arts. I can name numerous students over the years who arrived meek and mild, and left completely different people. The arts isn't always about being a performer, but the understanding of teamwork, personal development, and the skills to thrive in the outside world. We also learn from personal experiences too, and you have certainly found your niche in the world. I and the rest of the team may have only been a small part of your journey, but don't forget, you were also part of ours too, and we thank you for that. We teach arts and performance for a reason, if some become performers, great, if some become husbands and wives and have families, fantastic, if some find themselves in something different and make achievements in life, like you have, then that's outstanding. The most important thing is that the arts help people, especially youngsters, develop in so many different ways. Your story is inspirational, everyone should read and know about it, and the fact that the arts has played a part and helped you become the person that you are speaks volumes. Just know on behalf of all of the team that taught you, we are all very proud of you. X

Lucy Francis– This is great to hear and I hope your confidence and self belief continues to grow and guide you to even more achievements. I always bang on about the many and varied advantages of studying acting in whatever profession students choose. The communication skills and interpersonal skills and perception are all key to being a successful, empathetic and mindful colleague.

I don't think they will ever know how much those messages in response mean to me but it's something I won't forget. There was a familiar pattern with them and it certainly shows their individual and collective passion as well as how they remember me.

My experience was never a waste and as a friend has said to me many times, I've turned my pain into a purpose.

Why crafting saved my life [June 2021]

Before I met my ex I was studying youth work at the University of Chester. I was in my second year when I got a part-time job at the local cinema to fit alongside my studies. I entered into a relationship with my work colleague who became the person who abused me for several years.

Abuse is progressive but looking back I can see the subtle signs that lead to the control he had over me. He controlled my work life and sadly I gave up my studies at University, there were many factors to this but the fact I worked at the same place didn't help. Things changed when I had children and we had to work different shifts, I was relieved as it offered space however after every shift I would arrive home to an interrogation. Things got worse when he found out I had given work colleagues a lift after their shift as it was on my way home, he would refuse to sit in the car for 24 hours because they had sat in his seat. Eventually I reduced my working hours to just 4 hours a week and hardly had any money.

At the time a friend of mine was expecting and as a gift I decided to make a nappy cake, I was always creative so I thought I would give it a go. It followed with a friend of hers asking if I could make one for her for a fee, that's when I opened up my first business and this was the key to my freedom.

Despite why I set up the business it offered me the opportunity to be creative and I had so much enjoyment from this. At the beginning stages of a business you do everything and I enjoyed putting together graphics of my work.

The business gave me a focus and an excuse to be in the dining room away from him on an evening. I started networking with people online and grew my Facebook page to 4,000 likes in just over a year. I went to craft fairs and didn't care that he wasn't going to support me by looking after the children, I took them with me and juggled it all.

But it was the mum's in business gatherings that gave me the confidence and motivation to take the first step out. We separated but lived under the same roof and I got a part-time job to build my income to be able to have the money to get out for good.

If I hadn't explored my creative side with crafting then I wouldn't have started the business and wouldn't be where I am today.

Sexual Coercion [February 2022]

Some years ago I spoke at an event hosted by Min Grob of CCChat Magazine. I heard Dr Emma Katz speak on something I hadn't heard about before "Sexual Coercion". It has taken me some time to digest what I learned that day and also to accept what had happened to me in my abusive relationship.

Let me get into it...

Coercive control is an act or a pattern of acts of assault, threats, humiliation and intimidation or other abuse that is used to harm, punish, or frighten their victim. (Source: Women's Aid).

After 9 months of fleeing my abusive relationship, I had come to terms with what I had experienced, that I was a victim of domestic abuse and more specifically coercive control. I still hadn't understood how deep-rooted this was and I had felt that as a wife it was my duty to please my husband, therefore I hadn't accepted that my sex life had come into this equation.

Sexual coercion is unwanted sexual activity that happens when you are pressured, tricked, threatened, or forced in a nonphysical way. (Source: Women's Health).

As I mentioned, Dr Emma Katz talked about this very subject at the event and it was my awakening of coercive control being involved in my sex life.

Some of the ways I was sexually coerced:

Asking if I can ask the midwife when I can have sex after having my first child despite having forceps, I was pressured to have sex sooner making the healing process longer and having to see a gynaecologist.

My ex spoke to my best friend at the time and told her that his sex life is non-existent, knowing that she would come and inform me to apply pressure on me.

My ex said how can he not look at other women or flirt with them when he doesn't get any at home.

Me having to put in my digital diary to have sex with my ex at least twice a week (ideally three times a week) so that he doesn't instigate.

Doing the above meant that I would prevent what was going to happen if I didn't satisfy his needs, he would have sex with me in my sleep and I would wake up to him on top of me. At the time I felt I deserved what happened to me because I wasn't performing my wifely duties and the rape was a consequence of that. I didn't actually realise it was rape for years and this ultimately made me realise that I wasn't just a victim of emotional abuse but it was in fact physical as well.

The definition of the word rape:

The crime of forcing somebody to have sex when they do not want it or are not able to agree to it. (Source: Oxford Learners Dictionaries).

How this affects me today...

Sexual intercourse and intimacy are something I struggle with when it comes to having that time with my husband. I have had flashbacks during sex, I used to wear a top and couldn't be naked and I still sleep in fetal position at the edge of the bed. Thankfully I have an understanding husband who is always patient with me and never puts me under pressure. It's not easy though because I still have this clock in the back of my brain thinking about the last time I had sex with my husband, wondering when I need to do it again, the longer I leave it the more I feel my own pressure to get it over and done with.

I am actively working on my healing for my sex life and intimacy but there's no quick fix. I know I need to be kind to myself and I know I should be enjoying it myself.

Sharing this with you makes me feel vulnerable but I want others to know that rape doesn't always look like a random attack in a street or is a physically forceful incident like the stereotypical view we may have as a society (I include myself in this). I feel the way I was coerced to have sex and punished if I didn't is insidious and it still haunts me today.

That one friend [September 2022]

Let me take you back to your school years for a moment.

In your class do you remember the token teacher's pet, the popular kid, the sporty kid, the band geek, the loner or the bully?

I'm guessing that you can put faces to those labels, does the bully stand out to you the most?

Those first friends make a difference to our lives, sometimes they are the first relationships we make outside of our own family as a child. Those relationships are the ones where we decide if we want them in our lives or not, but how do we know if they are a good friend to have?

I know I didn't know, my teachers told us to apologise to one another when someone had done something mean, "make up and be friends again". Just because we are in a class together does not mean that we are all going to make good friends for one another. In adulthood we learn the hard way that we are not everyone's cup of tea, perhaps we eventually let it go or some of us may still hold onto the quantity of friends for validation.

What if the message was different? What if we were equipped with the tools to learn what a healthy friendship was? That we don't have to be friends with everyone in the class but we are respectful to those who we don't feel are a good friend for us?

It wasn't until my eldest daughter Sophie had that 'one' friend that wasn't healthy for her to be around. Sophie was only young and in Primary School, I was frustrated that she couldn't see why the friendship was disrupting her, hurting her, giving her anxiety and making her feel ashamed of herself.

Do you remember that 'one' friend that encouraged you to get into trouble, pressured you to do something you didn't want to do, took things from you, gossiped behind your back etc. Plus your parents knew they were a bad influence on you, so you didn't listen.

I could see a lot of similarities between my eldest and my younger self. I became worried about this becoming a repeated pattern and it was important that she knew that she didn't have to be liked by everyone or be friends with everyone. I knew that telling her wouldn't be the way that she would learn, she needed to discover what makes a healthy friendship and what makes an unhealthy friendship for herself.

The Funky Frecks was born, I wrote it with her and my younger self in mind. The draft was written on a train down from Hull to London in almost one sitting. A bit of editing later, I asked Sophie to read it for me as a first children's book. "Sam sounds like Abbie from school" she came up to me after reading through it, we had a conversation about why Sam wasn't a good friend to Jess in the story. I then drew two gingerbread men on paper, one was the perfect friend and the other was the friend that's not a very good friend for us. Sophie listed qualities she would like from a good friend and did the same on the other side.

The story opened her eyes to the different behaviours and the discussion alongside the activity I created took it further. Sophie started to look for the right friends and now has an amazing supportive friendship circle. Going forward my hope is that this has equipped Sophie for every relationship she makes, a preventative measure for unhealthy relationships.

The Funky Frecks educates through a form of entertainment, when you buy the book you gain access to a resource pack which can be used within your own conversations / youth groups / school classes / assemblies etc. Let's equip our children with the knowledge of healthy friendships, they deserve to have the best circle of supportive people around them just like we do.

Reflection on 'Learning Through Self-Education And Courses' [2024]

A mental health nurse shared with me a metaphor when I had a breakdown in 2023, I was feeling very ashamed of all the work I had put in to myself and had a complete relapse.

Imagine a Kaleidoscope and in each segment there are several different colours but there is only one red piece. In a Kaleidoscope they all reflect the same pattern but let's say ours doesn't, when you turn the scope all the patterns move around, the colours in each segment are in different places but then there's this one time that all the red pieces suddenly match in each segment. The red pieces are each of your different traumas and this is what happens when you have a CPTSD episode. All your individual trauma's come to the surface and it overwhelms you, this is understandable, you haven't relapsed.

The mental health nurse completely validated me in that moment and every time I learn more about how the trauma has affected me the more I am equipped in life. I don't remember the name of the gentleman who helped me reframe this on that day but if I have a lot to thank him for.

It didn't stop there, I said to him how I felt in my relapse, that I would have thought I'd be able to prevent these episodes or be able to make them less. He then mentioned a popular band and how they had developed but I didn't quite catch on until I thought about Taylor Swift. Taylor Swift has brought out music in her own seasons sometimes adapting to what the media and music industry wants: country, country pop, electronic and rock, pop, indie folk, indie rock and more into the sub categories. "Taylor started with country and that's a part of her journey but there are moments where she switches from country to rock, not ignoring the past but evolving, it's like different chapters of life. This is what you are doing, you aren't on your debut album anymore but look how far you've come to get to this point".

For some unknown reason, I felt the shame slowly lifting from my shoulders, it weighs me down quite a bit and hits hard when I am starting to feel unable to ground myself.

They say knowledge is power and in this way it has given me the ability to look at what's in my control and what isn't.

Examples of what's in my control:

My words

My mindset

Being present in this moment

How I speak to myself

What I give my energy to

How I spend my free time

How I move on from failure

The boundaries I set

The space I need

Examples of what's not in my control:

The actions of others

The outcomes of my efforts

Past mistakes

The opinions of others

What happens around me

What other people think of me

Other people's boundaries

I will never stop taking the time to develop my knowledge, work on grounding techniques and trying to remain in the present moment. What album could be next?

Mental Health

The 'real' me [January 2015]

Today is Blue Monday and I touched a little on this last week, if you haven't heard of Blue Monday then in a nutshell it is meant to be the most depressing day of the year.

So I am posting the 'real' me and I've splashed it right on the top image for all to see. I have to say I hate seeing this photo of me and sharing it with you is even more cringe worthy – I am going to explain why.

Let me first of all inform you that in the photo I am in my comfy clothes and I am wearing minimal make up if any at all. I have no foundation on, this is why you can see my current spotty skin. I have had a lack of sleep, perhaps only getting 2-3 hours a night.

I have been walking around every day like this for over a week, I felt that there was no point putting foundation on to cover those spots because it will only aggravate them and take longer to get rid of the outbreak. I am in comfy clothes because I have been unwell and for quite some time, I felt like I deserved to be comfortable with months of struggling in pain. Although I feel like hiding my face and hope not to bump into anyone I know.

So, why do I hate the way I look in this image? I don't think its actually how I feel? I believe its the world of media and how I feel I 'should' look. I should wear tight skinny jeans and I should cover up my spots, we are constantly shown on adverts how to cover up and how to look our best. At the moment I don't feel like I want to, I am so tired and even taking time to put make up on seems like a rather big job. I wouldn't usually admit this to anyone, let alone write this in a blog.

BUT... I feel it is important to share this with you. You are allowed to wear comfy clothes and no make-up if you decide. You are still beautiful, you don't have to be afraid of society or what people think, you are allowed to simply be you. It reminds me of watching Bridget Jones Diary when Colin Firth says "I like you veraly much. Just as you are", that's what we need in our lives.

Now you have seen the 'real' me, does it change your opinion about me?

I hope the answer to this is not because that's what it should be.

Wherever you are today and whatever you look like on Blue Monday, you are beautiful the way you are.

Do you doodle? [September 2018]

I used to love to doodle and I also fell in love with art when I was younger. Both of my parents were very artistic, my dad was a sign writer in his early years and sketched as a hobby. I took to it in school and did it as a GCSE, I found art quite therapeutic and one my favourite pieces of artwork was my final piece for my GCSE Project. It may look familiar as our task was to take a section of a piece of artwork and make it our own, put our own spin on it.

It said a lot about me back in those school years, my life seemed to be full of upset and I found my younger teens a big struggle. I made it through of course.

I am a visual person and if a lesson would lack visual learning I would drift in my thoughts, writing notes used to help but sometimes it would drift into doodles - throughout school, collage and university. Going into adulthood that side of me left, I suppose I don't sit in lessons I am disinterested in and anything I go to is something I am passionate about OR perhaps I forgot OR grew in my own self. Who knows.

I once did this sketch as a letter header of the golden snitch from Harry Potter.

BUT the other week I was put into a frustrating situation and I really found it a struggle… I had a pen and my post it note pad near by to take notes. That wasn't going to happen. Doodling made it very manageable as it stopped me from interrupting, getting angry and taking things personally.

I thought I would share the doodles with you…

What do you think?

What helps you when you are feeling frustrated/stressed/upset/angry?

Changing mindset [February 2020]

There are parts of my life and my experiences which I haven't been able to share and late last year there was no exception. I could share how I felt; I was stuck on my own on a train crying, trying to hold it back, sniveling and feeling very hot and bothered with no tissues to hand. But, I couldn't share why this came over me.

I find this difficult to handle at times because I know awareness of the emotions that link to certain situations would help others as well as myself. I have learned to project in different ways and even starting this journey I knew it wasn't going to be easy. I can say that going down this path wasn't easy and there have been times I have wondered if I can continue. Don't worry, I am not going anywhere, its more of an overwhelming feeling at times.

Usually, I am good at managing myself but it was bad timing on this train and I was a few hours away from my destination. I couldn't control my emotions, I am not saying I should either. I was ready to throw in the towel and questioned everything I was doing, only for an hour or so. It passed and I remembered to allow myself some time, to never act on emotion.

The next day and my whole mood changed, yes still emotional and stuck in my thoughts but with a different attitude…

I cannot give up.

I remember reading something a little while back that successful businesses are those who are able to work their way through difficult times and I felt it was the same for people. Last year I listened to a talk by the general manager for Fuji Film UK at the World Marketing Summit and it really brought that home to me. Fuji Film are known for their film reels for camera's, I personally remember taking the film reels to the shop to be processed and was very fond of them. In fact, I had a necklace with a miniature film on it that I won on a holiday when I was around 10. Photography went digital and you can imagine the impact it would have on such a business. Fuji Film changed and adapted to this new era using their specialties in different areas including scanning machines and anti-aging products. Hearing the journey they have taken and that they used a period of depression to learn and to find a new path was inspirational.

What sticks out though,,, they didn't pack up, they rode the wave. I think a lot of us hop from job to job and business ideas because we are expecting something big to happen fast. I can partly blame social media for this and that's why it's important for me to share some raw honest feelings of mine at times. I have mentioned before that my husband has said to me "you've got to go through the hard times to know what the good times feel like", sometimes you don't want to accept this but I believe that's pretty accurate even if it's hard to accept. I also believe that if you are going to find success then it is going to be in whatever you do and that hopping around isn't going to help you succeed, again the success is measured by each individual.

The talk from Fuji Film won't leave my mind anytime soon, it helped me personally but with my work as an author and advocate; and also with my husband's business OuTFox.

My mindset has improved over the years and it's only with self-development and putting tools in place for when I am feeling overwhelmed that aids my journey. The fact that I was able to shift my mindset within 24 hours of this moment I experienced is a success, years ago this would have knocked me for weeks and I wouldn't have moved in that time.

How do you help to work on your mindset and has it changed over time?

My Journey Into Long-Term Therapy: #No-MindLeftBehind [May 2024]

It's time to be brutally honest today and talk about my journey into long-term therapy, bear with me.

In August of 2023, I finally managed to secure long-term therapy for my CPTSD and I've been quiet with regards to writing about domestic abuse, almost silent. I have managed to keep up with some of my social media presence but if I'm honest I have had to focus on myself.

Before I started this new therapy, I had experienced several accesses to mental health support. Let me go back to when I was twelve, I had a Connexion counsellor at school, the reason behind this was that I was being bullied severely and the conclusion was that I was the problem (apparently). Unfortunately, a lot of my problems weren't just with school bullies but at home, I was unaware that my parents would get a detailed report of what I had said during these therapy sessions. You can imagine what difficulties this created, more so with my mother.

I'm sure you can see why I have had a negative view of mental health support with an automatic concern over trust for any mental health interventions thereafter.

I tried to battle through it on my own with the support of a healthy partner. When I entered University all that I knew about life came crumbling down. I disliked the cliques and the ostracisation of one of the friends I had made, I ultimately had to make the decision to be friends with her over the group of friends we were a part of. I learned a lot about unhealthy people and started to look deeper into my own relationships. Fellow University students would go home for half term to see family or their relatives would visit on campus, not me; I went to my boyfriend's house or stayed on campus on my own. I wondered why my family was so different from others and I felt like I was missing out, whilst a part of it felt normal another part of it felt abandoned. This led to my own version of rebelling, I went out drinking with different groups of people and on my own, I partied hard and locked myself in my university room with a box set of 24 (a TV show that was heavily popular at the time). From childhood, I was used to my own company and could keep myself busy so I managed through the first year.

However, it was during my university years that my healthy relationship ended and I fell into a relationship with a man who led me down a path of isolation through his manipulation and control tactics. I removed myself from family and friends almost completely. I ended up in my first round of counselling because all of our relationship problems were my fault, the counsellor identified that the relationship was an issue and couldn't help me. More time passed and I went to a different counsellor because I needed help and I needed to solve it, this one opened up the space for us to go together, thankfully he didn't turn up because the repercussions of this would have been incredibly dangerous. We passed a marriage "course" despite him not attending a couple of the sessions and me disclosing concerns and we did get married.

Unfortunately, my mental health support was very little even when I tried to take my own life. I sat in A&E being told I had to wait the hours for a mental health nurse to say I was OK to leave otherwise the police would arrest me. Not what I thought would happen in my moments of distress. My ex-husband had driven me insane and I had resulted in hurting myself and looking for an exit. I learned to dissociate more than I had done before, I played his game to survive and my two children were my reason to stay. I was a full-time mum and started to find my feet in how to work his system but the amount of damage he was creating was unknown to me at the time.

Once I had fled, I accessed my local GP and went straight onto antidepressants / anti-anxiety medication and remained on them for two years. There was no talk of accessing talking therapies but I self-referred myself to a programme that gave me access to a domestic abuse support worker. I also accessed tonnes of self-help, a family support worker, my bank and had more support from a new partner and his family. I didn't see it then but I was lucky at this point in my life despite finding everything incredibly difficult in dealing with the police and the family courts. Being on the medication and struggling with my mental health as a result of the trauma I had experienced led me to be an unreliable witness and so the police case that was open on the four different crimes he was arrested for was closed, that was a long four years.

Another four years go by, I find myself struggling again and this time I accessed a talking therapy to avoid going back onto medication again. I was limited to twelve sessions and one problem, I had to give it a shot. I did get on with the person I was assigned to but it was just by luck that she had past work in the domestic abuse sector to be able to support me. I was too complex for the one problem assigned to the 12 weeks because my CPTSD meant one trigger could unlock several different memories that I needed to address. It was exhausting but I got through this part of my life in which trust was broken, deceit was created and abandonment was eating away at me.

Another few years went by and I had a life-changing realisation followed by the diagnosis of ADHD, my life had turned on its head. I had settled down in my marriage and felt I was happy only to recognise my feelings for women that I couldn't ignore, this led to an identity crisis and a mental breakdown. I tried to escape my life on two occasions, one more serious than the other and I felt I had failed at being a 'survivor'. I'm still here today which means I am still a 'survivor', what I mean by this is; I had everything together and I couldn't cope with what was unfolding for the next part of my story.

It was at this point, in total crisis, that I accessed the emergency mental health service and I finally got listened to. I had to report to them weekly and they called me almost every other day to check on how I was doing (AKA checking my risk to life). Minutes in my day felt like hours, hours felt like days and every moment was a battle to just to carry on living.

After a couple of months of being with the emergency home care team, I was referred to long-term therapy which is for those with complex trauma. I shared my anxieties about therapy and questioned why I was only getting the help for this now after a decade of struggling since I fled my abusive ex-husband, a number of mental health nurses I had seen each said "I'd slipped through the system". I was reassured that this therapy was for my complex trauma and again I told myself to give it a shot despite feeling very sceptical.

I'm around 8/9 months into seeing my therapist almost every week. The environment is right, my therapist is right and reassured me that she is there for at least two years so she can really get to know me and give me the help I deserve. I pay a contribution payment of £10 per session which I'm more than happy to do because it has repaired my lack of trust for any therapy/counselling I've had in the past.

It has not been easy and it's really challenged me to think about how my trauma has truly affected my thought process, my decision making and me as a person. I give myself time around the session to prepare and then digest what we've spoken about. I come away feeling lighter but also validated in my feelings, tools to help me when I'm anxious or have triggers and I feel like I'm getting somewhere. My therapist had said I'm emotionally knowledgeable, I'm very self-aware, I'm able to reflect on myself but not emotionally resilient- this is what we are working on.

I'm not going to lie and tell you that therapy is a simple process because it isn't, you have realisations outside of the therapy sessions, the hard work comes outside of that session and you have to put the work in. Some weeks I feel I've moved forward a step but then another week I've moved back two steps. Remember, healing is not linear.

I'm on the path to assessment for AuDHD, I have an appointment in a couple of weeks and my hope is that I will be able to understand myself better and validation on how my brain works.

Mental health matters and without the right support it can deteriorate and feel very isolating. This month is Mental Health Awareness Month, if you're struggling then please reach out for help because the right support for you is available once you find it, persevere, self-refer and don't give up.

Mind has a Mental Health Awareness Week each year called #NoMindLeftBehind, if you haven't been on Minds website then it is most certainly worth a visit with lots of information and resources.

Thank you for being patient with my lack of consistency on my blog posts and social media. Just know, I am working on my next steps.

Reflection on 'Mental Health' [2024]

It may be the smallest chapter of the book but that's because mental health spills into the other chapters, how can it not?

Often mental health is seen as a negative statement but times are changing and when we look at mental health it's actually a scale, good mental health to not so good mental health. I find this allows us to talk about it in a less daunting way but it doesn't negate from the fact that there is still judgement at times.

I have had to work hard to get to where I am today and this work doesn't stop, I believe we choose our hard in life:

Being poor is hard | Being rich is hard

Choose your hard

Being unhealthy is hard | Being healthy is hard

Choose your hard

Working for a boss is hard | Being self employed is hard

Choose your hard

Not communicating is hard | Communication is hard

Choose your hard

I went to watch the film *Twisters* (2024) and one of the characters talks about how a tornado takes from people's lives but how long it takes from you is up to you, how long are you going to let it take from you?

I think about how much the abuse I was subjected to has taken from me, not just in the time but also in the weeks, months and years after. It still takes from me at times today and I have to fight so to work with that trauma, to quite the response and to work on not being in survival mode for a lot of the time.

"You don't face your fears, you ride them"

With this in mind, surviving wasn't an option it was the only choice I had. My mental health is affected by this is just a part of the damage from what happened to me, it doesn't mean I can't work to rebuild from it.

However, there are unfortunate times in which having a normal response to a traumatic experience becomes a problem. I sought help for my mental health just weeks after fleeing the relationship, I wasn't sleeping and I was living in the fear that he would find me so it felt like I needed to do something about it. I went to my local GP and I was forwarded to talking therapy but also placed on some anti anxiety/depression medication to help whilst I waited. The fact that I was prescribed this medication made an impact on my criminal court case meaning because there was minimal evidence they were relying on me and because of this medication it automatically made me an unreliable witness.

In fact only 5% of reported domestic abuse cases ended in a conviction as found between August 2022 and March 2023.

I have heard a number of people inform me that CPS haven't been able to take it forward because their medical history was required and they have had some sort of support for their mental health after escaping. Whilst this is an assumption, I know Dr Jessica Taylor had spoken about this at an event I was sharing the stage at, Domestic Abuse Prevention Convention by Kaleidoscopic UK 2022. I'd recommend looking at her work with Victim Focus to find out more about the studies she does if this is of interest.

I recognise reading something like this could put people off reporting but it's still important to bring it to the attention of the police. I know that I wasn't the only victim and even if nothing came off it in my case, it could build a picture of the character of that person to the police and they could be convicted at a later date. I often think of the statement "they were known to the police", it appears in documentaries or news reports. We can only do what we can do in line with the law.

I don't regret getting support for my mental health because not getting the support would have been a much worse outcome in life for me. I know that getting the right support at the right time has allowed me to open up doors that I saw where stuck closed for me before. I still find it a challenge and still have to work through my bad days but I have good days that really make it worth the while.

I'll keep focusing on the journey, not the destination.

Life After Domestic Abuse And Healthy Relationships

A conversation [August 2016]

Earlier today I was traveling home from a long weekend away and I stopped off for some drinks and snacks (as you do on a long journey back). I happened to be wearing my "Block the road to Isolation Junction" T-Shirt, comfortable clothing for the drive home.

I had selected some light snacks alongside a few cold latte drinks as I seem to have a sweet tooth for these and are refreshing in the hot weather we have been having. I pondered over to the checkout and the man at the checkout was really polite and friendly. I didn't catch his name as I was mindful I needed to get back on the road and I was taken a back by the conversation that came. After the usual weather discussion you have with people you don't know he asked me about my T-Shirt. For some reason I didn't say it was about the book I was releasing and I simply said "Its about a book that is due to be released in October and the core of it is about Domestic Abuse". In reply I received the raised eyebrows and the quite often unexpected surprise, followed by a long pause.

I didn't know what else to say in this pause but then he opened up to me and explained as part of his AA meetings he had discovered he had been abusive, the AA group supported him to build up the courage and apologise to his ex girlfriend. I have to admit I was really taken aback by this, 1) because I'm used to talking to victims and survivors and 2) because he opened up to me. He went on to tell me that he has been alcohol free for eight years and I said my polite well done's and I said to him to keep going and thanked him for sharing with me. This guy was so calm about talking to me about it and he wished me well and that he was going to look up Isolation Junction. We said our goodbyes and I have to admit I was surprised by all of this.

If there is a chance you are reading this then can I say it must have taken courage to talk to me today but I think it was very brave. I wish you all the best for the future and I hope looking further into my book and especially the that is running right now will show you that you taking that step was not just a step but a life changing event.

I will be wearing my T-Shirt on more occasions, you can get a T-Shirt like mine through pledging on the Kickstarter campaign.

Not only have I spoken to hundreds of women who have been in abusive relationships, and who have opened up to me. Now conversations are taking part on the other side of the junction as well. This book is already encouraging so many other conservations (and not just with me)

Short sharp poem challenge [May 2017]

Hull City of Culture (2017) was certainly a year for us Hullensians to celebrate. Throughout the year and on each Monday a new challenge is presented, people from Hull have been joining in.

"No Limits, our learning programme, aims to discover the creativity hidden beneath the surface in our fantastic city. We have teamed up with 64

Million Artists and community groups and organisations across Hull to set a weekly creative challenge to encourage everyone in the city to try something new – "

Last weeks was to write a short sharp poem and you can read more about these challenges on Hull City of Cultures official . I didn't write a short piece but I was in fact inspired to write a poem, I haven't written a poem since my teens so it has been a decade but I wanted to share it with you. It was written to my husband Rob who has been a huge support to me, you can also read more about our journey in the .

New, loved and no bars

I never thought that I would find,Someone who loves me back and is always kind,For I was lost and you found me,You broke me free from what bound me,You helped me learn to love again,To trust and open up and have no shame,You're my hero and knight,And now I want you to know that you don't need to fight,You don't need to hold me up when I feel so much pain,Because now we hold each other's hands and through this turmoil we have gained,A love that is so strong, unbreakable and pure,One that can stand tall and be united to endure,Thank you from the bottom of my heart,And thank you for showing me that I could have a new start.

I decided to read this out to Rob in which I welled up and struggled to get through it, it came from the heart.

Funnily enough whilst writing this and looking at the website I noticed that the week 1 challenge they featured my entry. I have to say I was delighted as I hadn't noticed or seen this. I am proud to be from Hull.

Domestic Abuse: Learning To Love And Trust Again [June 2017]

Taking those first steps back into the 'real' world after moving on from an abusive relationship can be very disconcerting. Those first few months bring to the fore the realisation of what you have just been put through and finding the confidence to make informed choices for yourself requires resilience and courage. It is certainly not easy and I personally spent a lot of the time questioning myself and my decisions. Who can you trust? Who can you talk to? Can I see my friends again? Will someone be watching me? Am I doing the right thing? Do I need someone else's approval?

I was very lucky to have found a friend in my (now) husband. He really didn't have it easy when we started our relationship. In fact there can be still moments now that I struggle to feel relaxed and confident. Ultimately, he helped to pick up the broken pieces and spent a long time in helping me to put them back together again. Make no mistake, it wasn't simple and there's no instruction manual or picture to refer to. He spent a lot of time guessing and trying to not make a wrong step as I worked my way through some fairly complex issues. I know if you asked him he would tell you in a heartbeat that it was worth it, but even I can see just how much he had to go through to earn my trust and to be able to put aside my negative thoughts of the past. Having a 'friend' has helped me enormously on the journey to being the person I always knew (deep down) I was but who had been hidden from sight by the effects of an abusive and coercive relationship.

In trying to offer some help I suggest that if you're trying to support a survivor that these steps may help:

1. Listen

2. Try to understand - don't make the other person feel unusual.

3. Keep calm - it's going to take time and most likely months if not years.

4. Actions speak louder then words - if you make those promises then stick to them.

5. Be affectionate - Often this is not paramount in the abusive relationship and affection is important as it releases the positive hormones, builds trust and reduces stress. Find out more.

6. Take things at his/her own pace and not force him/her to move on with the relationship faster, sexually or emotionally.

7. Playing devils advocate - in an appropriate away as this allows him/her to realise how they are coming across, examples include asking permission to go to the toilet, when/if they may eat or speak to friends.

In my opinion without trust there is no love (in its broadest sense) and without that there is no foundation for a healthy relationship.

One of my favourite quotes of all times is: 'The greatest thing you will ever learn, is just to love and be loved in return'. When I was in the abusive relationship I never appreciated what this really meant and I felt that I was giving everything of me to my abuser but I was ultimately gaining nothing back.

Thankfully as time moves on, more ways of addressing abuse are being developed such as The Domestic Violence Disclosure Scheme. This gives members of the public a 'right to ask' the police when they have a concern that their partner may pose a risk to them or where they are concerned that the partner of a member of their family or a friend may pose a risk to that individual. If an application is made under the scheme, police and partner agencies will carry out checks and if they show that the partner has a record of abusive offences, or there is other information to indicate that there may be a risk from the partner, the police will consider sharing this information.

Moving forward is hard and sometimes the abuse will come back in dreams, flashbacks, conversations or in other ways. I find that sometimes it feels like I am in a mental fight not to assume my husband is similar to the person who abused me. Years on and the moments have become less and I am able to shake it off but this has taken patience and has at times been mentally quite tough.

So my message to you today is that you can learn to love and trust again. The road may be difficult and sometimes challenging but its worth it!

What does freedom mean to you? [December 2017]

As part of my slot in this years online pop-up book shop event the other week I asked everyone what freedom meant to them.

The reason why I ask is because I never appreciated what freedom truly meant until I left the abusive relationship I was in. In fact when I came out of that relationship at first I had a time of withdrawal because I was so used to being told what to do and restricted on everything else. I didn't know what to do with myself and so I admit I went out on nights out and enjoyed myself, some might say I reclaimed my youth back. It has taken me a long time to feel comfortable making my own decisions but I have to say I enjoy making them now. At first I found it overwhelming having choices and at times now I don't want to make some decisions but the ones I do I thrive for the next. One I struggle with is spending money, I used to have to grovel and try and ask in a certain way to be able to spend money on gifts for occasions. I find that now I want to have no cap and the first Christmas not in that relationship I went wild, I spent on my family as I felt I had to make up for the years I was very restricted. My struggle now is to have complete mental freedom but it is still better then the prison of a home

I had before and so my mental fight to have a clear mind, that freedom is even more important to me.

So here is what freedom means to these 10 connections:

Hi Jen I have both of your books and myself have experienced similar things you and others have, freedom means everything. It is like a huge heavy weight inside your heart and on your body has being lifted. Just simple things like been able to eat or leave the house without anxiety was a weight lifted. Thank you for taking the time to share your story and others stories too. xxx

Suzanne Tanner

Freedom for me is being able to have fun with people I enjoy spending time with whenever I want to do that

Michelle Childs

Freedom to me means that I have made the right choices as I have made the bad ones before

Fiona Burnham

For all to live in harmony and support each other no matter what you are, where your from or your beliefs are. Each person is as valuable as the next and deserves the room to flourish. We also owe it to each other to Stand with and speak up for those who can't. Freedom is about all that and also being able to question without fear what is happening in our world. We need to encourage, educate and allow communities to grow and support each and every person be they young or old, male or female,

Richard Judd

Freedom means being able to be yourself, without being criticised or made fun of, without walking on eggshells, not knowing what to expect.

Helen Pryke

Choices!

Penny Buchan

For me, freedom is quite simply just owning myself and not having the worry if I'm living incorrectly!

Catherine Broster

For someone to give me a hand + knowing what path to take in life been down too many

Joela PortPow

Freedom to me means I can do what I want to without being judged good or bad for it and looking at how it benefits everyone not how negative effects take

Victor Wright

Freedom to me is the ability to own my decisions – whatever consequences that may hold. To know my life is mine, and if I choose to share it that's on my terms x

Heather Benstead

Please do write what Freedom means to you.

Hi Jennifer, Freedom, for me, means the ability to make my own decisions and make my own mistakes, dealing with the consequences, good or bad. There are things in my life I have no control over, like everyone else, but, I think that is the point of life. You shouldn't be able to 'control' anything besides yourself.

Jackie

For me freedom is independence; to make a choice and be able to do it without having to ask and be able to do what is right for you without comeback from others.

Kate Kenzie

Freedom for me is not only the financial freedom to walk away from my own poverty but to also have the ability to help others. Not being able to help makes me feel chained up ????

Haven

A love letter from me [February 2018]

It's Valentine's Day and for those who are abused it can feel like a very confusing day with a possibility of gaining some nice love and attention from their abuser, perhaps not knowing whether the other side is going to make an appearance instead.

If you recognise what I am saying then this is for you…

To you lovely lady,

If you haven't been told this for a while I want to let you know that you are beautiful, you can be who you want and most of all you are worth it.

If I could give you a voucher to be who you want to be, what would you do with the voucher and would you cash it in?

Would you change your hair colour? your clothes? personality? career? or where you live?

What would you change?

I used to dream about a happy family, affection, feeling butterflies in my tummy rather than spikes of anxiety. I didn't think I would ever feel happiness again but believe it or not, I did!!! I finally got my dream family lifestyle and I feel safe, secure, loved, cared for and I get to make my own choices, wear what I want, travel, speak to who I like and most of all be who I want to be.

I encourage you to take my voucher and to seek your happiness, because you are worth it. I may repeat myself here but I want to tell you that you are beautiful, there are people around you that think a lot of you (whether that's family, friends or a support worker), you are valued. I value you and you deserve the best. You are not alone, there are many who are going through the same and there are many who have found their happiness, you are not alone.

I want to wish you a happy Valentines day and send you all the love I can virtually.

Let me know if you claim your voucher and what plans you have if its safe to do so.

Lots of love and best wishes

Jennifer

A Survivor

The lasting effect of domestic abuse [February 2018]

I'm writing this at the happiest I have been in years. 2018 is my year and I'm taking it with a strong grip.

Years ago I left an abusive relationship I literally had what I could grab, I wasn't allowed to go back and get any of my further possessions and my abuser refused to give me anything after (even if this included photographs from my childhood), despite asking. I watched how he sold most of my beloved things on Facebook, most that I had spent an inheritance on. At first I was upset and angry but then I realised that I didn't really want my possessions back because they were stained with sickening memories, and that he gladly wanted to use the furniture for years and I am pretty sure he still has some of it now.

I came to my new house with my husband Rob (at the time he was my partner) and the rooms of our house were empty. There was only what we needed; a bed in each bedroom and some storage boxes for some clothes. I was fortunate to have my partners family and mine give us those beds in our bedrooms, a dining table, some clothes, cutlery and dishes etc. I will never forget just how much his family and mine stepped up to help in my time of need, the most desperate time of my life. Living without a washing machine for six months was very interesting and I am sure you can imagine how frustrating it became. We were without a sofa for quite sometime and sat on some blankets on the floor which developed into a blow up sofa and then into a second hand sofa. Looking back at the photos above upsets me, they are a horrific reminder of what I went through and what I lost. Not only did I lose my possessions I also lost many friends, I didn't really lose them but I had to disconnect from everybody that was connected with him- for our own safety.

If that wasn't enough I had a lot of debt from the financial abuse I sustained which was about to grow substantially over the next years, you wouldn't believe just how much solicitor fees grew.

The abuse I suffered equaled into years of hardship and continued abuse after the relationship had ended, I won't go too much into this now but I want you all to know that abuse doesn't finish when the relationship does. Usually for someone who has just left an abusive relationship that is when she is in the most danger.

BUT...

Two books later and standing as an advocate to those who are in abusive relationships...

2018 brought the year that we paid off all the debt we had including the large solicitor's bill. We had some help over the years from a couple of inheritances as well as family, without those I don't know what would have happened and my words cannot express my gratitude.

We are finally making our house a home, something that I've wanted to do for so many years.

This year we have bought some new homely things, two lovely armchairs and a sofa, a TV and sound bar, a handmade farmhouse style bench table, a grand mirror for our large lounge, a shoe cabinet which acts like a side board in the hall, some lampshades, a mirror for my daughter's room, a fish tank for my son's room, some photos finally custom framed and we've wallpapered the living room chimney breast. Next we are getting some handmade cushions and a Roman blind which is going to look so pretty.

I am finally feeling that my dreams are coming true. I have my dream husband, my dream family and the dream life which I always wanted. Soon I am going to have a dream holiday which will be a holiday of a lifetime.

I want to say that It's worth the years of striving, it's worth the years of embarrassment, it's worth the years of struggling, it's worth the sleepless nights, it's worth the fight, it's worth the years of never giving up despite the pain and the heart ache, it's worth taking it step by step and little by little – not thinking about what's completely out of reach because each day brings you closer to your goal.

If I can do it then anyone can do it. It may be years after that relationship has ended but it was never going to heal itself in weeks or months. I urge you to keep your focus. Keep your mind set. Keep your cool. Because doing this will ensure you keep your goal and will finally look back and see how far you've come- just like I can finally do.

And...

We even celebrated with a lovely breakfast at our new table (of course we've protected it with a cover) and enjoying our family life.

Imposter Syndrome [October 2019]

I wanted to share with you a section of my journey I have struggled with but feel I am overcoming little by little.

Let's go back to last year when I received the award for Most Informative Blogger in the Annual Blogger Bash Awards 2018. First of all, I couldn't believe I was a finalist and I questioned whether I really was informative. Second of all, at that time I didn't have the money to go down to London to not win and that was purely my thought process. I didn't think I deserved to be there and I felt it was through luck that I was in the finals. I didn't go and I didn't personally receive my award, I was so angry at myself for not going but understood why I went through the thought process and tried to make reasons as to not attend. In that moment I promised myself I would not do that again.

What is imposter syndrome?

Impostor syndrome refers to an internal experience of believing that you are not as competent as others perceive you to be. While this definition is usually narrowly applied to intelligence and achievement, it has links to perfectionism and the social context.

To put it simply, it is the experience of feeling like a phoney—you feel as though at any moment you are going to be found out as a fraud—like you don't belong where you are, and you only got there through dumb luck.

Late September this year and I find out I have been shortlisted for the Social Day: Social Media Marketing Awards 2019. I went through the same thought process, the first thing I did was look at who else was shortlisted and that's when I felt like I shouldn't even be in the shortlist at all. I was honestly impressed by all the names on the list and I only took a quick glance. To stop myself from preventing myself from going down to the Awards I quickly booked the tickets, hotel and travel. I remembered that I wasn't there last year at different awards and that I didn't want to be that person again, I changed my way of thinking and thought of it as a fantastic networking opportunity and thought of all the awesome people I would get to meet.

It came to the night and I made friends with Fiona Catchpowle who was on the list of finalists alongside me. Fiona was a delight to meet and get to know, she talks about menopause in the workplace and also is a digital marketing coordinator for *Henpicked*. I met some brilliant people and our table was celebratory of each other as we had a few winners on our table, that always helps keep the pace up. I only knew a few faces from attending the Social Day conference earlier this year so it was great to be welcomed.

It came to our award and I was feeling in a daze about it all, it could have been the wine as well. I was so happy for Fiona when she gained highly commended for the award and she owned it as she walked down the stairs,

I admired her confidence. Suddenly the lady next to me was giving me a nudge, I didn't hear my name and looked up to the screen to see my name but it didn't register fast enough. I must have been the longest walk to the stage, I was honestly in shock and trying to pose for a photo wasn't easy as I had this stunned feeling as well as wanting to cry. Fiona was there waiting for me at the side and gave me this huge hug telling me she knew I was going to win. I was so glad to have her there as she kept me going and we shared the interview together, I didn't prepare anything because GUESS WHAT I didn't believe I would need to.

Steps forward can often feel like giant leaps but they are filled with small steps forward and it's worth working on. This is just one example of how I have felt like an imposter, it doesn't help that I am a perfectionist and that you hear terms like 'fake it until you make it'. I am starting to learn to be proud of my achievements and this one I am overwhelmingly honoured of. Keep on overcoming because it will be worth it in the end and live for the moment you are in.

Life on Pause [November 2021]

Whilst I was in an abusive relationship I felt my life took a giant step back but it wasn't until after I left that I recognised the damage that had been done. It was more than life been on pause, I would say I was stuck like life was on repeat each day. I didn't grow, I became an empty shell and my career was certainly on pause. I had no idea what was going to happen with my life and I thought I was going to be left to suffer for the rest of my life.

The trouble with this is that I had a lot of time to think. I wondered about the friends I had and lost, old connections, old boyfriends and old work colleagues. Not only was life on pause but I couldn't move past my headspace to life as it was in the relationship, I wanted to go back in time. I didn't realise what an impact this would have on me going forward in life after abuse.

Grief and loss needs more conversation because not only is this present in losing someone we love but it happens through situations like being in an abusive relationship or separation.

I'm several years out of the relationship and I still think about those I used to have a connection with. I wish I hadn't lost contact, wish I hadn't pushed them away, wished I had the closure I now want. I pine for those I had in my life and the old life I could have had.

I have tried reconnecting and there have been different responses to this but I can safely say that I have held onto thoughts more than them and for many years. I wondered what happened to them, what they were doing now and if they ever thought about me (even if it was just a fleeting thought).

Expectations make this difficult because I have played out the scenarios of reuniting with them over in my head, but it's not reality or perhaps what they want. It means that I am feeling that loss all over again.

You might be thinking, why are you doing this then?

Well, I think I still need closure and I don't want to be in this middle void of not knowing if there could be a chance of friendship or simply taking up some of my headspace.

It's not an easy process, it's painful and it's challenging but ultimately this is growth for myself so I can move forward and not trap myself in the past any longer. It's not a good place to be and it can take over my mindset.

I remember when I made my first re-connection, I was invited to an event in Leeds as a farewell for an old colleague. I think I had been out of the abusive relationship for one or two years and I didn't think about the implications on my expectations or how I would feel. I endured the meal and got to see how everyone was happy, when I left, I sat in the car for an hour crying and feeling distraught.

A few months ago I found out that my ex-fiancé's mum had passed away and it was a few years ago, I had no idea. I was with him for 5 years and he was my fiancé before I met my ex-abuser, she was like a mum to me and I had always wanted to reach out to her, now I don't get that chance and I shouldn't have left it so long. It opened the door to attempt to get through a long list of reunions.

How can I manage my expectations with all this in mind?

This is an incredibly difficult task in itself but ideally I need to be realistic and not have any expectations at all.

What am I going to do to move forward?

I'm sad to say that I am taking you on a 360 journey because I have decided in this moment that I need to officially say bye to reconnecting with those people. I need to accept the loss and stop the pretence I have created in my mind. It makes me angry again about what my ex did to me, how much he stole from me, what I lost and how he forever has changed me. I am also not the person everyone knew before and they could have their own expectations.

Queue the song *Happily Ever After* by Billie Eilish on repeat and away I go.

It's OK because I am going to make new friends and be surrounded by those that accept me for who I am today. It sounds simple doesn't it? But, it isn't for me. However I have discovered that I have been through so much in my life that I can say "what will be will be" and nothing can surprise me, upset me or damage me. You can't break something that is now unbreakable.

Saying this, I have made friends who do understand me and I didn't realise that I would be so close to them. Kelly Smith is one that stands out to me, we recently met in London after four years of tweeting, Kelly flew all the way over from Texas.

This whole life on pause realisation has led me down a whole new path of self-discovery and I am now finding out who I am in a completely different light.

Are you an old friend of mine?

Please don't reach out to me in pity or because you've read this because I understand that time has passed and you may have witnessed my disturbing and uncomfortable journey. Just know that you have a place in my mind and I thank you for the time that you spent in my life. I miss those days and I will never forget them.

If you have a friend who has experienced domestic abuse they may be feeling the way I am. I know I am not the only one feeling this loss over and over again. Perhaps reaching out may be helpful to them, what's there to lose when so much has been lost already?

Are you a new friend of mine?

You are a friend of mine for a reason, I don't trust easily anymore and so you hold an important place in my life. Thank you for accepting me for who I am and creating new memories.

When you think you are almost there with recovery and a remix happens. This has been incredibly difficult to swallow.

Identity Crisis [February 2022]

In 2021 I went on a path to put myself first, put my own oxygen mask on before doing everything else. It was the most challenging thing I turned around in my life as I am so used to thinking of everyone else first, I came last. I didn't expect that this would actually lead to questioning my whole identity as a person.

I didn't really start putting myself first until around August when I realised I had done a pretty rubbish job at the New Year resolution. I would still ask permission from my husband to do something or search for a reason as to why I am doing an event/activity (EG for work or family). I just couldn't help myself but I knew I wanted to discover my independence and to be able to make my own decisions.

One day I woke up early and saw a post about a local Abseil which was less than a week away. I really wanted to go ahead and do it and without thought, I booked a place. When my husband (Rob) woke up, I told him what I had done and he was so surprised. The day came and I was in the first group to go down, I just did it! It was completely out of my character and I felt amazing, I was in control of something that was out of my control.

It didn't stop there, I decided to get myself a PT and work on myself. At first, it was because I was placed on a waiting list for an operation and about my health but as I started weight training I could see the benefits. Within 12 weeks I was deadlifting 110kg, I felt strong and powerful.

But then I discovered a quote that has stuck with me until this day and it really knocked me.

"Unlearning abuse also requires for me to unlearn the survival tactics I learned in abuse that I now call my personality. That's not who you are.

That's who you became based on who they were. Because pain builds WALLS but healing builds DOORS".

I have no idea why it has taken my eight years to realise that I have done exactly this and that my husband has met the person my ex created, he met me at my weakest.

I recognised that I have so much to work on, recover from and grow more. Just when you think you are there another box opens. I have to admit that it was a massive plot twist because I started questioning everything that makes up me as a person including my sexuality. I found this very difficult due to the sexual coercion and violence I had experienced, I thought it might be linked to the trauma. I spent November and December pretty much dissociated from life and everything felt very much tunnel vision.

It has taken four months to really come to terms with who I am and think about who I want to be. I considered the social person I was before I was with my ex and I thought about reclaiming the old me, I missed her. It wasn't right though, yes, I need to draw from that but ultimately I wouldn't be that person now if I hadn't gone through the abuse.

I heard a song by Luca Fogale called "Unfolding" and this really helped me to take my time and accept that I am truly unfolding. I am still finding the new me but I know I am already feeling better in myself, those around me can see the difference and I am excited about what the future holds. I've settled in my sexuality and just recently shared that I am a Bi Lesbian which has been the most challenging part of my journey so far.

I will be continue to embrace what I have found within myself from my 2021 resolution. I am never going back. I will never stop surviving.

The Anchor [September 2019]

I made it back from my solo holiday and I managed to write a few pieces whilst I was away. Going away was all about taking a step forward and recognising my healing process, you can read more in the blog post Solo Holiday Healing. I want to share with you this piece which I wrote when I was thinking about what grounds me.

The Anchor

You are the reason I keep going

The purpose I focus on

You bring light to my dark

The beat to my heart

You give me direction

The punch in the fight

You make me feel whole

The way I gain clarity

You are the anchor

In 2021 I experienced a feeling of being outer body despite being in my body. I recognised my emotions but didn't feel them, my mood was up and down, I made decisions that I wouldn't normally choose. I went through this for almost two months and I can look back and recognise when it began and when I came back to the surface. I now know that I was dissociating and I have come to learn more about it so that I can try to help myself when I go into this space.

Dissociation is a mental process of disconnection from your own thoughts, feelings, memories or sense of identity.

Signs of dissociating can include:

Finding yourself 'losing time'

You find yourself going 'outside your body' in times of stress

You feel emotionally numb

The world around you doesn't feel real

Dissociating usually develops through coping with trauma and most often form in childhood, children subjected to long-term physical / sexual or emotional abuse.

(Credit: Better Health Channel)

I can look back in my life and see where I have dissociated but I wasn't concerned about it, I thought they were episodes of depression at the time. Unfortunately the last year of my life I have been going in and out of this state and I feel my brain is trying to protect me. The amount I have gone through In such a short time has really woken me up to the self awareness I have developed. I feel I am unlocking a different kind of healing, perhaps before I was simply just getting on with life thinking that I was recovering from the trauma I have experienced, how wrong I was. I hadn't realised that I was still living out my survival tactics despite leaving an abusive relationship and going into a healthier one, since living on my own as a single person I have seen the depths of the abuse I endured and how I was institutionalised.

I feel that there are different levels of dissociating, from day dreaming, zoning out mid conversation to staring completely into space and not realising hours have passed you by. There are times I don't feel dissociating is harmful and that's when I know I am going to go through something challenging and I know the best place for me is to dissociate, this could be major surgery, fighting a fear, having to keep face in a disagreement. But most of the time it's not something I can control.

There are a number of ways you can get support for dissociating, like CBT therapy, hypnotherapy and other therapies. I believe that therapy should be approached in a holistic way because not one therapy fits each person, just like we all have different shoe sizes.

I have decided to look into getting support for this because this state of mind scares me. I want to feel my emotions, I want to be present and I don't want to feel as though I am lost or on auto pilot.

Going on the solo holiday was a part of taking the time to ground myself and see if I could connect myself again. Join the puzzle pieces and give myself a break. I started writing this whilst I was on holiday because I recognised that I was still dissociating and I felt the child inside of me is crying out. I feel alone and that there's no clear path for me to go on. The one thing that grounds me when I am in this place is my children and I am thankful that they are my anchor through these waves.

As I explore ways to help me with dissociation, I will collate them into a blog post to share my findings with you. If you experience dissociation and have something that helps, please reach out to me. I'm hopeful that this will help others that also go into a dissociative space.

Signs you are in a Healthy Relationship [September 2021]

Of course, your partner makes you feel happy. You know you want to be with them for as long as you can. You know you don't want to lose them. You love spending quality time together and have created memories worth cherishing for a long time. But when it comes to a healthy relationship, it always goes beyond just the smiles and memories, as there are other things to consider. So, what exactly makes a healthy relationship? Here are some signs worth keeping in mind.

You are not afraid to open up

Almost everyone can mention some things or behaviours they don't like about their partners. No partner is perfect, but as long as you feel comfortable expressing what you don't like, that is a sign that you are in a healthy relationship. It is important to note that your ability to express yourself freely does not always mean that you will choose to. Some people choose not to speak for one reason or another. But as long as your silence isn't the result of fear, you should have no reason to be alarmed.

On the contrary, that should be a red flag if you find it difficult to speak up and inform your partner about the things you don't like or feel secure enough to be open.

You trust each other

Trust should go both ways in a relationship. And while some people believe that it is impossible to trust another human being 100%, trust is still an essential ingredient in any healthy relationship. You should trust each other in various aspects of your relationship like your finances, parenting style, faithfulness, etc. Multiple studies have shown that partners or couples who trust each other tend to feel more satisfied with and in their relationships.

You are free to display your affection or speak each other's love language

You should feel free to show your affection in a healthy relationship, whether in words or action. Just like the freedom you have to communicate what bothers you, you can also express your joys. Gifts tend to be one of the best ways to 'speak' where words fail. For example, you can invest in a Claddagh ring white gold variant as a gift to display your loyalty and the true love you have for your partner. Also, in a healthy relationship, you know each other's love language. Whether through gifts or physical touch, you know just the right love buttons to push.

You feel independent from your partner

You'll often hear some love birds express how they cannot live without their partners. As romantic as that may sound if you cannot feel independent from your partner, that isn't a sign of a healthy relationship. You are still two different people in a relationship, and each person needs to have and maintain their own identity independent from the other. That means you can have and enjoy your hobbies, separate friendships, and different interests while having some in common

Reflection on 'Life After Domestic Abuse And Healthy Relationships' [2024]

I think it's clear that life after domestic abuse is incredibly challenging with lots of hard work to learn how to live a life that is made up of your own decisions and be confident in those. Doing this for yourself is just the first step because when relationships are added in this is where things become more complex.

Relationships with family, friends, colleagues and of course romantic relationships. Each relationship requires energy and in my early years of "survival" once I had fled, I hadn't realised the impact the relationship had on my family members. It was only when a family member talked about the guilt they had over not being able to do something sooner for me or recognising that I needed help when I was in the relationship with an abusive person. Another family member told me that they had mourned the loss of who I was as a person, they didn't see me and when they did I wasn't the person I was, I'd come back from the dead as a zombie clearly.

They went onto explain that even though I was back, I'm not the same person I was.

Not only does it affect them but it had affected my perception on my family, the slow isolation from my family along with the manipulative comments that gave more distance confused me for a long time. I often felt like I had my abusers voice as a layer of conscience. It provided barriers and often led me to either submit and people please or cut communication and deal with the bare minimum communication. I couldn't trust my own thoughts.

Romantic relationships have been even more of a challenge but I'm glad I didn't give up on the idea of love. I will say that I find it hard to trust in any relationship and if trust is broken it's incredibly hard to rebuild. I'm thankful that I met my second husband, he helped me in ways I didn't think a human would help another and without him being in my life in the right place at the right time. Trust took years to grow and I look back an honestly feel for this guy because he went through it with me, not only was I surviving days after but he was surviving the support he gave me. Our relationship came to an end once I discovered my sexuality of which he supported and it was challenging for different reasons but I can clearly see that there is a huge difference between an unhealthy relationship and a healthy relationship. I'm proud of us both to be able to communicate for the children and we work together to do our best for them. He was always a friend before a romantic partner and it would be a shame to completely say goodbye to that.

Now I'm further down the line of recovery I feel more in control of my life and I'm able to communicate my needs and boundaries with a romantic partner. The trust issue will always be there but I can now see what I am in control of and what I am not in control of which gives me the independence to know that I will be OK no matter what happens. I own this life.

However, communication is imperative for me to be able to have relationships with people. Whether they are family, friends or romantic partners. I have to work on communication in terms of my own triggers and what I'm working through but I also need a level of communication from them in terms of reassurance, patience and willingness to try and understand. It means that it requires work from both sides but if both of us give the same energy then it matches and this results in valuable connections that feed the soul. I have a small circle that I give time to and they know me well enough to accept me as I am, I'm no longer changing for someone or putting my needs aside.

Support

A mum's experience of abuse [2017]

Having children changes your life in so many ways, not least because you acquire a protective instinct that makes you want to protect them from harm or hurt. I remember feeling this protectiveness instantly when my first child was born. I had never considered how I would feel but instantly I felt that protectiveness which made me want to keep her safe and protect her. This is a feeling which has developed for each of my three children as the term 'mother hen' now makes perfect sense to me!

One thing I didn't expect to have to do is to have to put up my protective barrier at home. Sadly, this feeling grew until in the end I felt anxious and aware 24/7 which had the obvious effect of sleep deprivation and its effect on my health, well being and actions.

Let me explain what I am talking about. To put it quite simply, I was in an abusive relationship. I didn't see it coming and a lot of people now ask me how I let it happened to me. I am an intelligent person and people wonder how someone like me could have let it happen. Was I unaware? thick? stupid? gullible? spineless? I guess this is what I want to make everyone aware of, as I am none of these things. Domestic abuse doesn't just appear overnight and it doesn't just ' turn on'. It happens over time and it increases in pressure, time and number of incidents that can be attributed to be abuse. It is like a snowball going down a steep hill. Over time and space it increases in size and speed until eventually it is out of control and it is difficult, if not impossible to stop.

You would imagine it would be easy to spot an abusive person but ultimately they are very manipulative and clever. However, I do wonder if I had of known the warning signs during the early stages then perhaps I would have recognised them and I could have stopped that snowball before it went out of control and nearly, so very nearly, destroyed my peace of mind and my life.

What is even worse is if you are trying to protect children from a situation like this. Because you are fearful of what will happen if you try to flee the situation, you feel trapped and in limbo. In fact, you believe what the abuser is saying and nothing else could be possibly be correct because all you have done is listen to them and try to fix things, make them better and eventually do as they say so that you can get through the viciousness of the cycle faster and reach the calmer stages.

I have to say if you don't know where to look for help I found that it is not very easy to access at all apart from going to a refuge. The housing offices couldn't help me as I was housed and as my abuser was classed as a tenant he couldn't just be evicted. The Social Services didn't help because from their point of view everything seemed fine. Solicitors charge for advice and you may or may not have the money. In the end the police are there and they can only take someone into custody for so many hours after an incident and then they are free to return home… that sounds like a good idea doesn't it?

However, I did find that the police are informative if you do want to flee and of course over the past couple of years the law has changed in favour of the abused. But now more than ever more awareness is needed on every level. Even you reading this will help you or someone else.

There are some things to be aware of in identifying domestic abuse:

Intimidation such as making you afraid and intimidating you using looks, actions and gestures

Using children by threatening to take them away or to relay messages, or making you feel guilty about them;

Using male privilege in a condescending way by treating you like a servant and being the one to define the role of men and women;

Isolating you from friends and family and limiting your outside involvement;

Emotional abuse such as putting you down humiliating you and making you feel guilty;

Threats whether small or large and financial abuse such as preventing you from getting a job or taking your money and not letting you know about family income are all indicators.

Need more help recognising abuse, see the refuge website on recognising abuse .

If you think you're being abused call the national domestic abuse line on **0808 2000 247**.

Thank you for taking the time to read this blog post and share it. domestic abuse effects 1 in 4 women and 1 in 6 men. How many of your friends could be going through it right now?

Thankfully, I am a survivor along with other survivors who are out there. Talking about it is hard but it does help. The snowball that became a boulder eventually smashed into smithereens and someone came into my life, together with my family and friends, as well as his own, they joined with me to pick up the pieces and to move forward as the confident individual I always was (deep down). Years later I'm still rebuilding my life but I recognise that I was lucky. You don't have to be a victim, you can be a survivor as well - all you need is that hope and some help both practical and in terms of building self confidence (whether that be from family or friends or the services).

Five ways I overcame hurtful memories... [July 2018]

Sticks and stones will break my bones but names will never hurt me...

How true is this? The fact is it does hurt and sticks with you for a long time, perhaps until you leave this life.

I recently shared one of the humiliating things my abuser used to say and so I wanted to give you five things you can do to hide away those memories, to replace a negative with a positive, to move away from the pain it can cause, to obliterate them.

Why do we focus on the memories that haunt us when we start to think positive of ourselves? When I come close to being confident I have this voice interrupt me at the back of my head saying 'just remember your smile'. For those of you who don't know I was in an abusive relationship and one of the tactics my abuser would use was humiliation, one of the items he fixated on was my smile which I never had a problem with before then. He used to point, laugh, he would even cry laughable tears at me and tell me to stop smiling because it made him laugh so much. What he used to call me made an impact on others because it made the reader think instantly of what they were once called.

Five ways I overcame those memories:

Listen to those who love and care for you. They will have their true opinion of you. If it's negative then they are not the person you are looking for with this. It has to be someone who gives you those nice remarks or motivates you to keep going, they are perfect.

Write five other positives for the one negative someone focused on. What do you love about yourself? What do you like? And if you are struggling what five things do other people say they like about you?

Tell someone you can trust, doing this will help it feel less like a burden. I went to the extreme lengths to sharing it on a blog post but the amount of response I received for sharing was incredibly helpful, reassuring and made me think the problem was never me. Seems obvious but it really helps not keeping it to yourself when it flashes up one day in your mind.

If you don't have someone to tell, tell me! I am happy to listen, we can get through these 5 steps. Or perhaps there's someone you can share it with that's completely not linked to your life, someone you see in passing each day? perhaps you have a life coach or a therapist? a support worker? family worker?

Go out and make that niggle shine! For me it was all about my smile and how it looked, I wear bright lipstick now, I show my smile off! Show it off because what that person didn't 'like' another with love!

Still not feeling positive? Give it time, write about it in a diary or a letter to yourself to open in a year. Read over it in a years time and does it still feel this way? Your body and your feelings and thoughts are yours, you can take ownership but it may take a little longer than others so don't worry if it takes a little more time.

These were just a few ways I have helped myself, they may not help you. Please feel free to share what helps you.

The biggest change in my life was finding the ability to love myself, it's taken years and I'm still working on it. It's hard to love yourself especially when there's a voice in the back of your mind.

We are all different and unique and we should embrace it, otherwise we would find each other boring.

You have got this!

Sleeping Tips [May 2019]

A while ago I asked my street teamers what kind of blog posts they would like. I was interested to know what would be said and I felt it was important to talk about what you want to read. One of the topics was to do with sleeping and tips on how to get to sleep if you're struggling. I have struggled a lot with sleep over the years and it isn't always perfect but these are the things I try to help on a bad day.

My tips:

Watch something funny before bed to take my mind of negative thoughts.

Listen to some relaxation or chill out music.

Read part of my book which is a book chosen for pleasure and isn't going to trigger any negative emotions.

A hot chocolate, get that warm feeling in your tummy.

Take a bath, If I start to get desperate I will take a bath, I don't like doing this but if I feel nothing is going to help then this is one of my last resort points.

Done all of the above? Try putting on a boring film in bed, usually this last step does it for me as I can't be bothered to watch it. It has to be something you are mildly interested in though, so be mindful of that.

There's another rule that must be followed when trying all of the above for me and that's not going on my phone. My phone will continue to ping through the night as people tweet and message from all over the world. Phone's are known to stimulate the brain and that's the last thing I want to do at 1am when I am struggling to get to sleep.

What helps you get to sleep?

Finding your why [January 2021]

Since my first book was published, many people have asked me why I wrote Isolation Junction. I suppose there are many answers to that question raging from, "Because I wanted to see if I could write at length" to "Because I wanted to think through how I felt about the topic." In order to write this article I have spent some time thinking hard about the answer to this question and I think that the most honest answer I can give is that I wrote 'Isolation Junction' because I believe I had a contribution to make to the debate about domestic violence and coercive control. In writing my book as a narrative rather than as an academic discussion paper I was hoping that it would appeal to a new and possibly different audience. Those who perhaps enjoy relaxing, reading a novel as part of their busy lives and who in reading the novel will relate to and recognise aspects of unacceptable behaviour.

It is my belief that often books which deliver the most powerful message are those where the message is hidden within the story. Why else would some of these stories hit the headlines as Hollywood blockbusters if their message was not compelling and powerful?

It is often said that everyone has a book in them and I believe this to be true. So, how do you go about recognising this and beginning your journey?

Here's a good place to start discovering your message or what to write about:

First list topics you're interested in, love or feel passionate about – this could be anything from a hobby to a taboo subject to an interest in fairy-tales.

Do an old fashioned spider diagram of aspects of the topic and include any thoughts for writing material. e.g. For me it was the taboo subject of domestic abuse so I wrote my passionate feelings on it : awareness, show abuse for what it can be like, focus on the emotional abuse and coercive control side as it needs to be uncovered, my fears, my sacrifice, women need to know about unhealthy relationships, what does a healthy relationship look like. A life changing message, education through entertainment. And so on...

Which of your topics has the most depth? Which one are you drawn to? Which one is screaming out the be wrote about? Which one has a message? The message doesn't have to be a life changing but it could bring someone an escapism, it could be that you want to help people through a self help book (how does it help?), it could be that you want to feed those who love fantasy (how does your idea bring something new to the genre). One of the common questions is why did you write your book? so it's great to find that why before you put pen to paper, fingers to the keys.

Keep all the spider diagrams in case you come back to them at a later date. Focus on the topic and spider gram you have chosen to write about and test it out, get some ideas together. Continue to build on the spider diagram and think about the basic wireframe of a book.

Write a short story, blog or even your thoughts about the topic and post it out to the world, ask followers, friends and family to give you feedback. If you don't already have a social media page and website then begin growing this right away. You can let people know that you're working on and gain feedback. Take on the feedback and rethink or build your idea. Making your why a powerful one.

Not only will this help the beginning of your writing journey but it will help your marketing because you can tell people why you wrote your book, blog post, short story etc.

Let me tell you a little more about my why that I touched on earlier and where the inspiration came from.

I was on an awareness course about Domestic Abuse. Alongside me were other women who had been in abusive relationships. As the day progressed, I found that I simply couldn't believe that some of what the other women were saying was exactly what I had gone through but just in a different format. Domestic Abuse tends to go in a cycle and whichever way it begins, the behaviour spirals again and again. At first it could be months between incidents but for me, as time went on there were many instances within one day. It is quite normal to try to prevent the cycle from starting again by changing your behaviour as much as possible. By the end of the course I had come to understand that we were all subjected to the same behaviour and that no one knew before that this could even happen to someone i.e. that a relationship can be so unhealthy and soul destroying. I realised that others simply needed to know more about this unacceptable behaviour; they needed to see the warning signs before the relationship goes further or the behaviour gets even more serious. On the other hand I needed others to see the behaviour for what it is. If people are in a relationship and the behaviour within it is not acceptable and is not their fault, it can't simply be changed by changing yourself.

I knew I had a story to tell and with my previous unfinished written work I realised my first novel had to be more than a book but that all important message – a way for others to be able to pass a book on to help victims and to get the penny to drop moment and bring about realisation of what is happening sooner. This means that when the relationship ends victims and survivors realise they are not the only ones out there and it's okay to talk about the abuse. But also uniquely in an 'entertaining' way and using a form of media and the work of fiction to bring it to light.

It didn't take long to get going as I had written a lot of notes about my own feelings as a way of releasing my emotions, I found the process therapeutic and as I started the journey I also brought my friends and family and followers on it with me. I set up social media FB page and Twitter feed early on to start sharing thoughts, updates, quotes, memes and links relating to writing, the progress of my journey and domestic abuse. It certainly made an impact and unfortunately a lot of messages from fellow victims and survivors of their own struggles and the feeling of not being able to talk about it until seeing my posts and messaging me.

Helping yourself to make the best decisions in life [August 2020]

In life, we face decisions on a daily basis. Of course, most of these decisions are relatively minor and inconsequential. They might include things like what you eat for breakfast, whether you walk to the store or drive or what outfit to wear on a night out. They're decisions that we make without too much thought, hesitation or consultation. But every now and then, bigger decisions will come along. We may find ourselves struggling with these a little more. But the good news is that we have some tips and tricks that can help you along the way!

I have had to make decisions that have made a huge difference in my life, in fact some I didn't think I would ever have to face. The most obvious one is finally leaving that abusive relationship I was in, I feared the worst and didn't know what would come of me, now I am happily married and aware of how it impacted my life. It took me many attempts leaving before finally getting to that point of not going back.

Now decisions can be hard for me to make because I was controlled to the point of being unable to make decisions for myself. I do find it difficult at times, especially if I am not focused. I certainly need to work on this area of my life.

I hope this collaborative post helps you.

Know What You Want

If your decision impacts your life or lifestyle, it's important to know what you want in life and whether following the path being offered to you will help you reach your ultimate goal. Sure, diversions are fine and you may change your mind as time goes on. But knowing what you want will often make decision making easier.

Consider Your Own Happiness

First and foremost, you need to take your own happiness and what you want into account when making decisions. So many people will make decisions based around others' wants and needs without ever questioning what they want themselves and what's best for them. You can't let your whole life revolve around keeping others happy and being convenient. Instead, weigh up how your decision will impact you and whether it's worth carrying out or not.

Consider Others' Happiness

Of course, if you have dependents, you will have to take their happiness and wellbeing into account too. You'll need to find something that works for everyone. Whether you have kids, pets or elderly or sick loved ones who need your support, you will have to weigh up their needs in regards to major decisions you make.

Seek Advice

Of course, many of us feel more confident in making big decisions if we have advice from others. So, seek advice and see what others have to say. Remember, their word isn't necessarily gospel. Instead, it can simply help you to see things from different perspectives, consider things you might not have considered yourself and more. There are countless sources of support out there. You could consult family and friends. You could take to online forums.

I personally look for advice in different ways and feel I know myself more now than I did before, do you feel you know yourself?

Weigh Up the Pros and Cons

Often, decisions are difficult because they come with both pros and cons. It's a good idea to create a list of both. This way, you can weigh up the pros and the cons of any decision you may need to make. Write a list with pros and cons. See which outweighs the other.

Something I have done many times before and it really does help me gain clarity.

Trust Your Instinct

You can't mull over a decision forever. You'll have to make a decision at some point. So, just go with your gut instinct if you find yourself taking too long.

These are just a few suggestions that could help you along the way. Different people have different processes. But hopefully, some of the above information can guide you in the right direction!

Reflection on 'Support' [2024]

Over the years I have accessed a number of support services, in the beginning I felt a lot of shame in needing the support but now I have come to accept that if I need help then just go and get it. I will get to where I need to be a lot quicker with some support as opposed to trying to wade through it on my own.

If you are fighting it all on your own and have thought about getting support but you've been stopped because of shame, this is for you, I'm going to go through the support I have had and list how it's helped me. You deserve to be supported in the times you need it and that there are services waiting to be there for you, you are not alone.

Domestic Abuse Support Worker - Accompanied me to every court case, interviews, meetings there were in relation to the events at the time. Directed me to further support services that could help, signed me up for courses she was a part of and run for women who have fled an abusive person. The support worker was a listening ear in the moment I really struggled with. They corresponded with the police and any other services to follow them up or if I didn't understand what was happening.

Family Support Worker - Looked after us as a family including sourcing a washing machine for us which was invaluable after four to six months living without one. Connected us with the community centre for supportive group sessions and drop ins for a range of different areas.

Local GP - Directed me to different therapy services knowing talking therapy might be the first step and leading onto anti anxiety/ anti depressive medication to relieve me temporarily from the stress that I was under.

Social Services - Listened to me when I had been reported as a "concern" and could see the bigger picture, reassured me and kept me updated on any further reporting.

Let's Talk - The original talking service commissioned by the NHS to provide 12 weeks worth of counselling, I was blessed to have had someone who used to work with those who had experienced domestic abuse which helped massively.

Brave Group - The group that is based on The Recovery Toolkit by Sue Penna ran for women who want to live their life after abuse and take those steps into their own future. This group changed my life and I often talk about it, I went on to meet Sue Penna and work with her.

Jigsaw - The programme that created foundations of parenting which I attended just because I wanted to show the court I was putting the children first in everything. I took some great things from this course and still use them today.

Police - The people who were there when I had to take the step to do something about what had happened to me including post separation abuse. It was certainly a postcode lottery situation but I was still met with kindness and an attempt of understanding. I was able to feedback and as a result there was a region wide training on language and communication with victims of domestic abuse.

Solicitor - Where would I be without my solicitor? I'm glad I scratched the money together and I'm thankful that they set up a payment plan for me in regards to my circumstances. I couldn't have done it without them.

Midwife - When pregnant with my third child and away from the abusive relationship they still checked in with me and gave me support with my mental health.

Local MP - Took my concerns over the Children and Family Court Advisory and Support Service (CAFCASS) complaints policy by supporting my concerns, unfortunately the policy is still in place to this day. I managed to get to a manager high up in CAFCASS and a response from the justice minister. Despite not having the ability to take this further on my own it was still recognised by my local MP and I had her full support and same frustrations.

Humber Wellbeing Hub - The wellbeing volunteers that operate on the Humber Bridge due to the increase in tragedies. They approached me when I was having a CPTSD episode and couldn't reach out to those who supported me and the phone lines were busy for the other services. I wanted to un-alive myself and stood for hours feeling drawn into the water, they supported me, talked with me and got me in touch with the emergency support services.

West Community Mental Health Team - Were there for me once I had been seen by the Humber Wellbeing Hub and continued to support me as a home patient for the weeks that followed it until we had a solid care plan in place with appropriate referrals. They made such a huge difference as I went in 2/3 times a week in person, phoned each day and slowly weaned off to once a week and eventually I was set up with the right therapy.

Psychology UK - Diagnosed me with my ADHD which helped me start to look for the right support to go forward. They were more efficient then waiting for the NHS waiting times and I managed to gain access via the right to choose option. I am still under them for the tritiation of my medication.

PIP - After nine months of waiting and an appeal I managed to get access to PIP to help me with taxi costs, medical equipment or services. This was in result to my three major surgeries in 2023.

Space2BeHeard - The therapy service that looks after me to this date, it's long term therapy with someone who understands the amount of trauma and the impact it has had on me as a person. They are their to help guide me but not give me the answers. This has been a life changing service.

University student support services - To help with my learning with CPTSD, ADHD and recovery from the major surgeries in mind. I am yet to receive the support on campus but I have managed to access the DSA which is helping me to invest in materials and software for my learning and transport.

I'm sure there are more than I've listed here but these are the main ones who have helped me in the past eleven years and not just with regards to the abuse I endured.

I wouldn't be where I am today without this support, it's almost like a crutch to assist you in your walking in times you are finding it difficult to take steps forward.

Here's another reminder for you that... you are not alone.

It's also important to have support from friends, family, partners, work colleagues or work places in general. The more someone has an understanding of your situation the better equipped they are to help, this isn't a prompt to share it with every single person you talk to but if you are struggling with something then it's better to make someone aware.

I have a small supportive circle and I also have a "professional" support circle like the therapist I work with.

Your support circle are those who are cheering you on as you run the marathon, they are ecstatic when you reach that finish.

Who's in your support circle?

Important Phone Numbers And Supportive Websites

If you have been affected by what you have read in this book, you are not alone, talking to someone is the first step to feeling less alone.

If you are in immediate risk from harm

Police: 999

None emergency: 101

If you feel intimidated, controlled or unable to speak out to your partner

24-hour free-phone National Domestic Abuse helpline (UK): 0808 2000 247

Or visit

If you need to talk to someone

24-hour free-phone Samaritans: 116 123

Or visit https://www.samaritans.org/

For a safe space to talk about your mental health

Mind Support Line: 0300 102 1234

Or visit https://www.mind.org.uk/

There are national, local, charity, and council-led helplines, so I urge you to make that call, if it's safe.

Visit Helplines Partnership for a full directory which you can search in: https://www.helplines.org/helplines/

If you are not in the UK, I am sure there are support lines of a similar nature so please make that quick search to find local help.

Lastly if you are wanting to reach out to me personally you can email me at contact@jennifergilmour.com and I will respond as soon as I am able to, please be mindful that my inbox and any social media pages with my name are run solely by me.

Or visit: https://jennifergilmour.com/

Where to next?

I'm publishing this fourth book in Domestic Violence Awareness Month (October) 2024 which is where I began eight years ago when I published my debut novel Isolation Junction and started my work on raising awareness on coercive control. It hasn't been an easy journey and within that time I have experienced more than most but I'm still using my best efforts to raise awareness and educate others through my lived experiences.

But where am I right now? What are my plans for the future? How am I going to move forward?

I'll get to that in a moment but I want to bring you up to speed with what has happened for me over the last few years.

First of all here's a timeline of memorable moments within my writing career.

2016 - *Isolation Junction*

2017 - *Clipped Wings*

2017 - #AbuseTalk

2018 - Most Informative Blogger Award 2018, Bloggers Bash Annual Awards

2019 - UK & European Award for Using Social Media for Good 2019, Social Day: Social Media Marketing Awards

2020 - *The Recovery Toolkit*

2020 - #SBS Winner, Small Business Sunday by BBC Dragon Theo Paphitis

2022 - *The Power of Letters*

2023 - *The Funky Frecks*

2024 - *Turning Trauma into Triumph*

Amongst these milestones I have lost a baby, struggled through lockdown, opened a community building business, discovered my sexuality, had a second divorce, single parenting three children, diagnosed with Adenomyosis and ADHD, three major surgeries, four procedures, travelled to five different countries and found a love for weightlifting (my personal best for a deadlift is 120kg).

My children are now fourteen, twelve and almost nine. This last year I have been emotionally tested in a multitude of different ways but I have my coping strategies and am still working on those when last year I unlocked the box on my childhood trauma, something I wasn't expecting. Having positive experiences within my weekly therapy sessions at Space2BeHeard in Hull I needed to find my independence and to be able to depend solely on myself.

After a High School Reunion which marked twenty years I started to reflect on my achievements and look to the future. Old school colleagues knew who I was and followed my story online and in the media, however I didn't know much about them at all. It made me realise what a difference I was making even within my old circles and I started to think about what direction I needed to take next.

Covid-19 made a difference to many lives and for me it meant that I had to concentrate on my three children and work on how to bring some money into the household. The pressure and stress alone meant that I didn't write properly for a couple of years and speaking events didn't really bounce back.

When I became a single parent I recognised that this was the time for me to relook at what I enjoyed, what I didn't and what I wanted for myself. It's often challenging to think about what your own hopes and dreams are when you are busy helping little humans grow, they come first. The mixture of financial panic and medical problems of 2022-2024 gave me permission to think about how I was going to give myself the best life and the kids would benefit, a happy mum = happy kids.

Unfortunately there are spaces where lived experiences isn't enough and there's a need for an academic qualification which I have always repelled after hearing feedback from professionals who had said they learned more from me than the textbooks.

However, through my therapy journey and talking about trauma on my TikTok I realised that once again my self education was helping others to get the help or support they need to live a life after a traumatic experience. This is when I realised how much time I had invested so much time listening to Dr's and experts on the impact of trauma, unhealthy and healthy relationships; I still had a need to learn more and to make a difference in some way.

With that been said, I started University in September 2024 to study a BSc (Hons) in Psychology with the view to fast track onto the doctorate after qualifying. Yes this may seem like a long road ahead of me but Rome wasn't built in a day and I know what I want to do with my research when looking ahead.

Back in 2009, I qualified with a DipHE and JNC in Christian Youth Work, I was due to go onto my third year which would make it into the degree I thought I wanted for my career. I never returned for my third year, I entered a relationship that turned abusive. Every year since then I have seen the students pass me by on graduation day and felt an overwhelming disappointing hole, especially as I had always been the 'geek' of the class. Yes I still have a passion for youth and children's work but it became an unsociable role. However, when applying for Student Finance England to be able to go onto the Psychology degree as a mature student at the age of 36 this has helped me: 1- I have the credits to get onto the course with two national diplomas under my belt 2- I haven't already got that level of qualification. The road for me was going to be a lot easier than if I had a degree and was applying to study another degree.

What does this mean?

It means that I believe it all happened for a reason, there was a reason I didn't complete the Christian Youth Work degree and I now don't feel so heavy like I have done for the last fourteen years that I have seen others graduate and not me.

I've discovered my passion through my path, my pain will be made a purpose.

At this point the old me would have said "I can't wait to graduate" but I can wait because I'm going to enjoy every part of my journey as I learn, as I grow and as I continue to hold myself in the present moment as much as I can possibly do.

You are never too old to start something new, to make a difference or to take on a new hobby.

Join me

You've got this far in my journey with me and now you can join me in my next steps forward as I work my way through the Psychology degree as a mature student. I plan to share my personal learnings, my every day life, the theories that grip me, the challenges of juggling everything, my lifestyle and anything else that links to my lived experiences.

Get your notepads at the ready, your pens in your pencil case and your travel mugs to hand.

Join me on Substack here: https://jenlgilmour.substack.com

I can't wait to see you there and please don't be shy, share your thoughts on my publications.

Acknowledgements

Thank you first to Carol Kerry-Green who has assisted with structuring and formatting of this book, Carol has been a great support of recent with my writing journey.

Thank you to the Writers@... group in Hull who have not only given their thoughts and views on how to structure this project but they are there for me weekly in my writing journey. I'm so grateful to have your creative support and friendship.

Thank you to book bloggers – without your support I would at times feel like I am talking to myself in the land of the world wide web. Never think your role isn't important because you motivate, encourage and inspire writers to continue in their work.

Thank you to fellow non-fiction writers who continue to inspire me and motivate me to continue in sharing my journey.

Thank you to readers and followers on social media, without your virtual support in engaging with my content then I wouldn't still be trying to raise awareness of domestic abuse.

Thank you to those that work in the domestic abuse sector that ask me questions about my journey, take an interest in hearing about my experience, are happy for me to ask my own questions and be challenged. You've allowed me to grow in different ways and without the encouragement and reassurance I wouldn't have been able to take the steps I am now taking to do my own research.

In memory of Paul

Paul Weatherill was very supportive of the work I did and the community projects I'd get involved in, it's only right that he has a special mention.

Paul discovered my work back in 2017 when he shared a photo of my debut novel Isolation Junction on his Facebook feed along with his thoughts on the book and tagged me in it personally. I was invited for a coffee meet to talk about the contents of the book, I accepted and I listened as he shared some of his experiences of supporting people who have experienced domestic abuse.

Every Kickstarter campaign that I have put out to the world, Paul supported. You will find his name in the acknowledgements section of my past publications. Paul would turn up to local events that I speak at, engage on social media, help raise awareness, stayed in touch and asked me what I was working on to be kept up to date.

One day I invited him to a community event I was putting together (Coffee, Cake & Craft) and he offered to make cakes going forward, each month Paul would come along with another delightful cake. Everyone loved Paul's company, he loved to share his stories with the group which had laughs, eye opening moments and peaked interest. If someone was feeling low he would be there with positive reinforcement, motivate others and put a smile peoples faces.

I'll never forget when he turned up to watch me abseil down the K2 building in Hull for a charity, he wanted to make sure there were photos taken for my record and cheered me along.

Support for my work doesn't go unnoticed, it makes a difference to my ability to keep raising awareness and to me personally. I will miss Paul's presence online, at events, in conversation and in general.

Thank you Paul for being unapologetically you, you will be missed.

Supporters, Backers And Pledgers

This book was originally crowdfunded on Kickstarter to cover the costs of formatting and marketing, but most importantly to give those who have followed my journey the opportunity to grab a copy before the general public. The campaign consisted of supporters (those who helped spread the word), backers (those who backed the campaign) and pledgers (those who chose a reward like being named in the following acknowledgements list).

Thank you to each and every one of you.

A special thank you to advocate:

Richard Graham Judd

Thank you to pledgers:

Antonella Barbuscia

Beat Mueller

Becka Simm

Bob Bennett

Bonnie Lacey

Carol Kerry-Green

Chris Hopkins

Elizabeth Wilkinson MBE

Hilary Banks

Janet Gilson

Jessica Page

Kris EGAN-LEIGH

Mary Metcalfe

Orna Ross

Katie Shepherd

Rachael Hawkins

Steph Hemsted

Tim Parsons

Tracey Carson

I have been self-employed for several years and have met many businesses and authors along the way. I know how important it is to be able to get your name out there and so I offered a business pledge on the campaign. Take a virtual stroll through the business owners and fellow authors websites who are working hard to get their name out there.

Thank you to business owners and authors:

DV-ACT - https://www.dvact.org/

Sarah Brason - Brand Amplifier: www.sarahbrason.com

Sara Goode - Wellbeing Mentor: www.saragoode.com

Jacqui Bourne - Purpose Unleashed

James Ballantyne - https://jamesballantyneyouthworker.co.uk

About The Author

Jennifer Gilmour is an author and advocate for women in abusive relationships, using her own experiences of domestic abuse as a catalyst to bring awareness and to help others. Jennifer has published two works, Isolation Junction and Clipped Wings, which have both been Amazon Best Sellers and received awards. Jennifer speaks at events across the UK and continues to raise awareness through blog posts, public speaking, radio interviews, and social media.

Jennifer has listened to her readers and has grown a digital community to support discussions about domestic abuse online. Starting with her Twitter Chat #AbuseTalk, which opened late 2017, this developed into an online forum in 2018. In 2019, Jennifer launched a podcast which includes interviews with those in the sector and gives followers the opportunity to ask burning questions.

Most Informative Blogger Award 2018 (Bloggers Bash Annual Awards)

UK & European Award for using Social Media for Good 2019 (Social Day: Social Media Marketing Awards)

Small Business Sunday Winner 2020 (Theo Paphitis #SBS)

Jennifer says: "Together we are louder"

@JenLGilmour

JenniferGilmour.com

Link.tree/jenlgilmour

References

Most of this book has been adapted from my original blog posts -

A couple of my guest posts have been adapted by the original blog posts - https://jennifergilmour.com/reviews-guest-blogs/

Huffington Post articles - https://www.huffingtonpost.co.uk/author/jennifer-gilmour

Kickstarter campaigns referenced- https://www.kickstarter.com/profile/jenlgilmour

For the publications I have written and referenced - https://jennifergilmour.com/my-books/

For the publications I have been a part of and referenced -

References within the new content added to this book

Clipped Wings (2017), Jennifer Gilmour - Book

Don't Be So Hard On Yourself (2015), Jess Glynne - Song

Twisters (2024) - Movie

Domestic Abuse in England and Wales overview: November 2023 - https://www.ons.gov.uk/peoplepopulationandcommunity/crimeandjustice/bulletins/domesticabuseinenglandandwalesoverview/november2023

If you are looking for something in particular and can't find a direct link, please don't hesitate to get in touch with me: contact@jennifergilmour.com

Also By Jennifer Gilmour

Isolation Junction

100 reasons to leave, 1,000 reasons to stay

When Rose married the love of her life she was expecting the perfect family life she'd always dreamed of, but before her first child was born her husband, Darren, changed.

Almost overnight Rose's life is turned upside down and the life she'd envisioned seemed like an impossible dream.

As Darren's abuse deepens, Rose has 100 reasons to leave but 1,000s why she can't. Will she ever escape the hellish life she and her children are trapped in?

Can Rose stop her life spiralling further out of control? Can she find the life she desperately wants for her children? Stuck at Isolation Junction, which way will Rose turn?

This second edition details the emotional abuse one woman endured before finding the confidence to try to regain her independence. A story many people find themselves in but one which few find the strength to talk about, Isolation Junction takes us on a journey through the emotional nightmare of domestic abuse with the hope it will embolden others to find the courage to speak out.

Clipped Wings

Just imagine you thought that you had met the man or woman of your dreams. This person was charming and you thought they were the one or perhaps that this was fate; it was just meant to be.

But as the months go by things start to change. Their behaviour towards you isn't the same, they are more critical, more particular about your appearance, what you do, how you do it, who you see. Months and years go by and you feel isolated from your friends and family because that behaviour has now turned into threats, maybe violence and you feel that your identity is all but gone. But still you stay. Where would you go? Who would help you?

The message of this book is one of courage, as with courage comes awareness and an ability to look back on your relationship and see signs you didn't see before, signs which signify unpleasantness, manipulation, and control.

A group of survivors have written, or been interviewed, about their own experiences. These accounts – in their own words – show that survivors do have a voice and that it needs to be heard. They show that abuse isn't unique or strange but that it is, in fact, a surprisingly common problem in today's society. With their help, we can reach out to educate people about this insidious behaviour.

It is unacceptable, unwarranted, and brings misery and disharmony to so many.

This book shows that survivors don't stand alone, in fact, 1 in 4 women and 1 in 6 men will suffer domestic abuse and/or coercive control … The problem is very real.

"Together, we bring our stories to you and sing out like a silent choir, to broadcast to the world that with courage comes awareness and with awareness comes the freedom that everyone deserves – to be themselves."

The Funky Frecks

Jess is excited to start her new school and she soon makes friends.

But it's not long before one friendship makes her feel uncomfortable.

Feeling trapped and alone, Jess isn't happy.

Can she figure out a way to ask for the help she needs?

Parents & Teachers: Downloadable resources included.

To help start the conversation about healthy and unhealthy friendships, there are some free resources which can be used at home or in group settings.

Printed in Great Britain
by Amazon